Dear Peter,

I made a little contribution to the MWB book. You made a huge contribution to my personal development. You also made me "popular" and sometimes "disliked" by IMD course participants thru the MWB case.
Thanks for your beautiful words in your column.

Defining Moments

Defining Moments

What every leader should know about balancing life

IMD
INTERNATIONAL
Real World. Real Learning®

Kees van der Graaf

IMD
INTERNATIONAL

Real World. Real Learning®

IMD International
Ch. de Bellerive 23, P.O. Box 915
CH-1001 Lausanne, Switzerland
Tel: +41 21 618 01 11
www.imd.org

First published 2011

Designed and produced by: BBH Solutions Visuelles, Vevey, Switzerland, www.bbhgraphic.com
Printed by: PCL Presses Centrales SA, Renens, Switzerland, www.pcl.ch
Edited by: Beverley Lennox
Photographs on pages x, 21, 23, 47, 51, 98, 99, 100, 108, 121 by: Nanning Barendsz, Bleiswijk, Netherlands

FSC
www.fsc.org
MIX
From responsible
sources
FSC® C081883

To Renée, Bart, Diederik and Michiel

Contents

Acknowledgments

Without Tom Malnight inviting me to come to IMD as an Executive-in-Residence, I would never have started to write this book. He stimulated me to write as many stories as possible, to download all my learnings and insights.

Renée and my sons – Bart, Diederik and Michiel – kept both my feet on the ground during my entire career – no celebrity behaviour was allowed. They constantly reminded me of my roles as caring husband and father. I love them dearly.

It was Antony Burgmans who had the confidence in me to give me more and more responsible roles at Unilever, which culminated in my appointment to the Unilever Board.

Beverley Lennox from IMD made my stories come to life, by her tough but excellent editing. The IMD team supported me in the realization of the book.

I was surprised to get so many positive stories from the "columnists". Their inputs brought more meaning to my stories.

I felt honoured that Paul Polman, Unilever's CEO, did not hesitate for a second when I asked him to write the foreword. Unilever has given me a fabulous 32 years. They gave me the space and the trust to fulfil my different missions in all my jobs. I was allowed to make mistakes, as long as I learnt from them. What a unique company this is! Long before sustainability and corporate social responsibility became buzzwords, they were already being applied at Unilever, from the heart and the brain.

The inspiring environment at IMD provided me with the energy and creativity to write this book. It is an oasis of academic rest. The 80 CEO interviews Tom and I conducted around the world gave me so many new insights. I consider it a privilege to have had this opportunity at the end of my career.

Thanks to all the other members of my family, my friends from all periods and my colleagues. Without you, these stories would never have happened.

Columnists

Foreword

Readers beware. This is no ordinary business book. But then the author is no ordinary businessman. As the personal stories and anecdotes in *Defining Moments* make clear, Kees van der Graaf is a man driven by a higher purpose.

In particular, he embodies the concept – recently embraced but for so long dismissed in business circles – of "shared value", the idea that a company has a set of responsibilities that go well beyond a financial return to shareholders. As he argues, business does not operate in a silo, but instead needs to reach out and engage with a much wider group of stakeholders in the common effort of making the world a better place.

It is this understanding that recently led Unilever to commit to doubling the size of its business while reducing its overall environmental footprint. Firm targets are set out in the Unilever Sustainable Living Plan (USLP). For the first time, we want to decouple growth from environmental impact. It's a new way of doing business, though it builds on a long history of shared value within Unilever, of which Kees was one of the key proponents.

In the wake of an economic and financial crisis that has shaken trust in business and undermined faith in business leaders, the idea of shared value is steadily gathering pace. And not before time. Given the search for a new moral and ethical compass, this book is particularly timely. The author was a pioneer in a pioneering company. It proved to be a powerful combination.

Above all perhaps, *Defining Moments* is a deeply honest, personal and at times moving account of one man's voyage of self-discovery. Through a series of "defining moments", Kees shows how personal crises and professional challenges can not only be overcome but can also be used to help give greater purpose and meaning to life – to help make the individual stronger, the family more cohesive and the organization more united.

The experiences described in this book may at times be raw, but they are real and authentic, and the advice Kees offers to future business leaders on the back of these stories is all the more powerful for that. As such, this account of a career that has had its fair share of ups and downs is worth any number of those theoretical books on the "do's and don'ts" of business that litter the shelves of bookshops and business school libraries.

Defining Moments describes what every leader should know about balancing life. It will make you smile, it will make you think and I also hope that it will make you act.

Paul Polman
Chief Executive Officer
Unilever

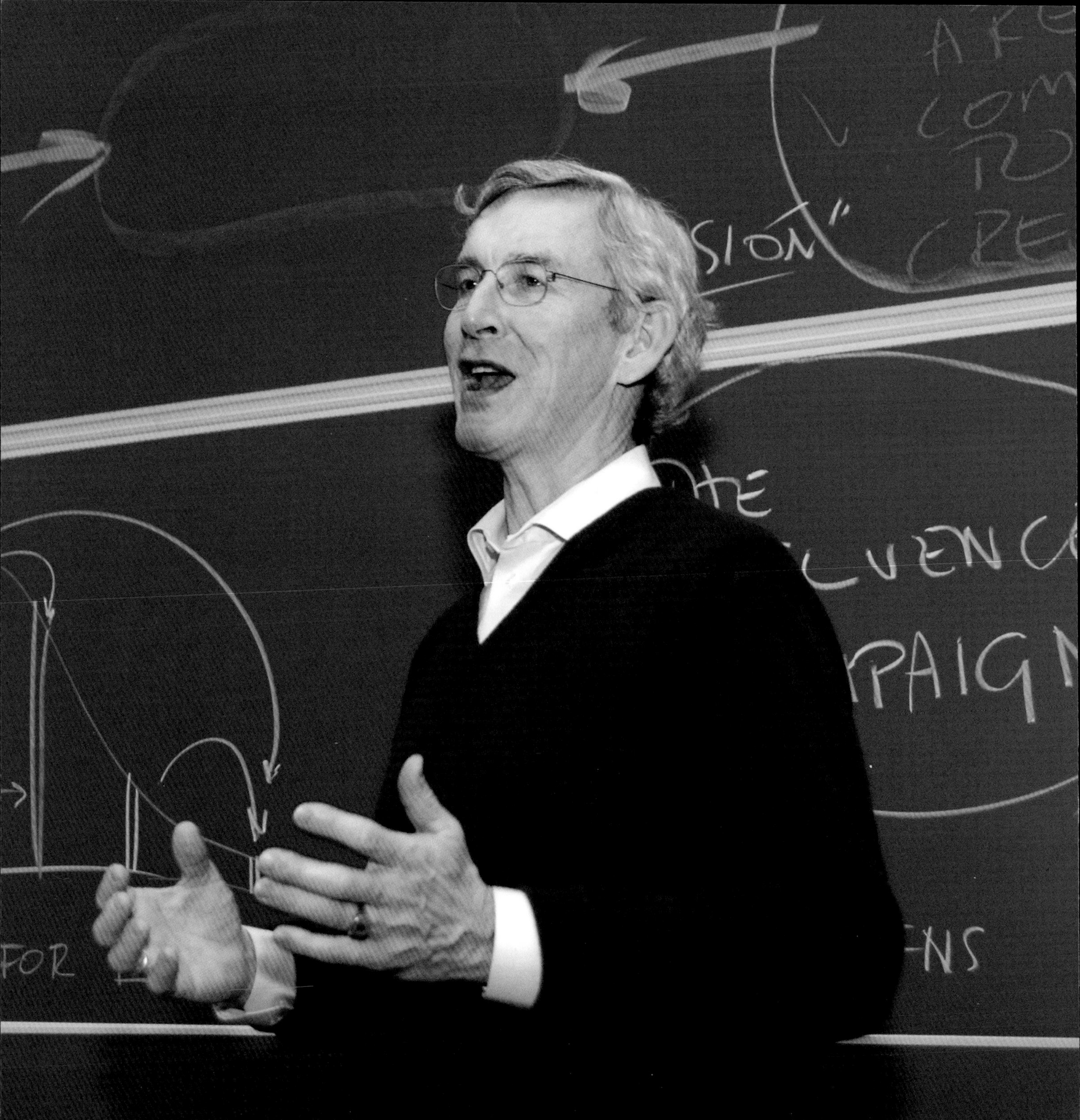

Preface

My life changed the day my oldest son Bart was diagnosed with FSHD – the facio-scapulo humeral form of muscular dystrophy. Until that moment, life had been uncomplicated. Unilever made the decisions about what we should do next, which may sound somewhat negative, but I really enjoyed working for this great company and the family loved our international experiences.

My career was moving fast – much faster than I ever dreamt it would. My ultimate goal was to lead an operating company for Unilever somewhere in the world. This happened when I was asked to go to Switzerland in 1993, but theoretically, I still had 22 years to go to before retiring at age 65, so I had to rethink my future ambitions. But, by far, the most important reason to rethink my future was Bart.

Bart's diagnosis in 1992 opened our eyes to a different world – a world in which we became less self-centred and more caring of others. As a result, my lovely wife Renée and I started the FSHD Foundation to raise money to fund research programmes to understand this rare disease. We also got involved in a number of other muscular dystrophy-

> *My aim is that this book will help generate awareness of FSHD, as well as raise funds for the FSHD Foundation – either through net revenues or future speaking/ teaching engagements for myself.*

related activities. A new balance began to take shape in our lives – the focus was shifting from being career-driven to being responsible for not only our children and my career, but also for our role in society. Subconsciously, I also began applying this notion in my roles at Unilever. I became aware that there was a real world out there crying for support from people who had the social position, the networks, the heart and, therefore, the capability and motivation to make a (small) difference. Words like social responsibility and sustainability began to have real meaning for me.

In February 2001, I met Professor Tom Malnight, from IMD in Lausanne, Switzerland. He had been involved with the two Chairmen of Unilever in designing a leadership journey to Costa Rica, the objective of which was to open the eyes of the 100 most senior managers at Unilever to a different way of relating to each other and to important stakeholders. Tom later helped me set up a major change process in Unilever Europe's Ice Cream and Frozen Foods business. For the following six or seven years, he and I worked together intensely to prepare the businesses under my responsibility for the future. In this period, I started to toy with something I called the "three-circle model".

Many people keep their family, business and society roles strictly separate. I have great difficulty with this approach because I believe the circles should overlap and that individuals should live in one holistic world rather than building concrete walls between their different roles in life.

By allowing my three different roles – loving and caring husband and father, Unilever executive and Chairman of the FSHD Foundation – to overlap, I was able to become more balanced and, therefore, more able to deal with the difficulties and issues that I was encountering in each of my different roles. The opposite is also true. When things go very well in one area, the energy garnered from that area spreads to your other roles, and as a result, you will be more effective in those other roles. In other words, if you view your roles in life holistically, I believe you will be more effective and you will be perceived as a more authentic person. The more authentic you are, the more respect you will earn from your environment.

One aspect that I initially overlooked in the model, which I later introduced, was the fact that you also have to look after yourself. In the last years of my career at Unilever, I engaged a personal trainer who would go jogging with me once a week. Unilever encouraged its senior managers to have a personal trainer because it is convinced of the importance of being in good shape. Since then, Pernette Osinga, a former Olympic fencing athlete, takes me out to the dunes once a week for an hour and a half of exercising. When you are in good physical shape, you can deal with significantly more stress. In addition to working out, it is important to follow a healthy lifestyle with a balanced diet. I am not suggesting dieting, just using a little discipline. If you practice moderation, you can still indulge from time to time.

During my last two years at Unilever, I was also introduced to self-reflection. I became much more aware of myself – my motives, my drivers and my deeper purpose. This helped me to make a few very important decisions, not the least of which was the decision to take early retirement from Unilever. This opened the doors for me to get involved in the *Power of Balance* project with Tom Malnight.

As I had been toying with my three-circle model with Tom on several occasions, he encouraged me to consider joining IMD as an Executive-in-Residence, as this would provide me with an opportunity to spend time developing my model. And so it happened that in November 2008, I took my place in the senior professors' wing at IMD. The concept was pretty straightforward. I would be paid for every hour of teaching in the classroom. The rest of the time, I could do whatever I wanted. And, it would be greatly appreciated if I could write a book during my time at IMD. I was supposed to stay a year. But a year became two, and it will probably become even longer. Why? I really enjoy the teaching part. But you can only teach if you have cases to share. So, initially, I spent a significant amount of time writing a few Unilever cases. The popular ones were about managing complexity, Unilever's corporate social responsibility (CSR) activities, managing change and the power of balance.

I also love engaging with the MBA participants, which has resulted in several coaching and career counselling assignments. The sensation of helping young people move forward is a rewarding experience. But the real reason for extending my stay at IMD is the ambitious research project that Tom and I have developed to understand more about the motives and drivers of executives. The aim is to be able to draw conclusions about their ability to create balance in their lives and to cope with the challenges they and their organizations will face 5 to 10 years in the future.

The project initially began when we asked the 2009 MBA class of 100 students to write us a story describing a moment in their lives when they felt really good, when things had worked out well for them and they were in control of the situation. In the next phase, we asked the same question of about 150 middle managers who were attending programmes at IMD. Later we interviewed some 80 CEOs and former CEOs (many of whom were non-executive board members) from around the world. They represented everything from large firms to major multinationals and conglomerates – both public and private – with family, private equity or state ownership.

We covered the globe from Brazil to China, visiting all kinds of industries and services. The two-hour interviews focused on how these leaders were dealing with the key challenges they were facing in preparing their organizations for the future, how they were dealing with different dilemmas and how they were preparing the next generation for their roles. We also spoke about the responsibilities of a firm vis-à-vis the environment and the impact of the company on society. They shared their successes and failures with us. Finally, we asked the 2010 class of MBA students what a company would have to do to gain their commitment to stay in its employ for a ten-year period.

All this information is now being digested, coded and analysed, and the resulting insights will be shared through a series of articles produced by the IMD Global CEO Center – Leading in a Connected Future (LCF) – which I will co-direct with Tom Malnight. The aim is to enter into a dialogue with senior leaders and, together with them, develop ways in which leaders can be more effective in the future. Most likely "balance" will be an important element of the findings.

Shortly after joining IMD, I was asked by Professors Jean-François Manzoni and Tom Malnight to give a lecture to a group

IMD Global CEO Center
Leading in a Connected Future (LCF)

The IMD Global CEO Center was founded in January 2011, based on the insights gained from interviewing 80 CEOs and senior leaders of organizations worldwide. Under the leadership of Co-Directors Tom Malnight and Kees van der Graaf, the center's mission is to contribute to creating long-term value for both business and society by inspiring and challenging senior business leaders to prepare for sustainable success in a volatile, uncertain and connected future. By capitalizing on its strong ongoing global research base, LCF will develop new insights and materials for senior leaders and help them apply new concepts in an effort to prepare their organizations for the challenges of the future. Specifically, the center will address:

- How businesses can actively contribute to creating a better world, while strengthening their own competitive positions to meet the ever-changing demands of the markets in which they operate.
- How business leaders can move beyond transactional interactions to build effective, mutually beneficial and trusting relationships with owners, society, consumers and employees.
- What top executives need to do today to move beyond a focus on short-term financial results to prepare themselves, their leadership teams and their organizations for long-term sustainable success?

The IMD Global CEO Center shares IMD's commitment to a "real world, real learning" approach, focusing on ensuring "real impact." It also shares IMD's core values, which emphasize open, pioneering and collaborative relationships.

of senior Philips executives. Jean-François briefed me on the programme and told me what he expected from my lecture. He is a real believer in the power of storytelling, so he asked me to tell him what had impacted me the most during my career at Unilever. After hearing a few of my stories, he said that it would be great if I could share two or three of them with the Philips group.

He was convinced that this approach would work well in getting a number of key learning points out to the participants.

insight

Storytelling is the best way to make a message memorable.

It was not difficult to convince me that storytelling is an effective communications tool. During my days as the President of Unilever Europe, the leadership team was facing the difficult task of telling our organization that we were about to embark on the biggest reshaping and restructuring exercise in its history. It was a difficult, complicated and tough message. Our Communications Vice President recommended that we deliver a consistent message to our people but that we do it in our own words with our own examples. To help us with this task, we brought in an outfit to teach us the art of storytelling. It was a real success. Instead of showing the standard PowerPoint slides and Q&As, each member of the leadership team told the story about Europe in his or her own way – it was a more humane and memorable way to deliver a difficult message.

Jean-François' Column

Powerful moments with Kees

Jean-François Manzoni
IMD Professor
www.imd.org

I have had the pleasure of watching Kees share some of his "defining moments" with several groups of senior executives. In fact, I was there the first time Kees ventured into this territory. I remember the first time, and every time since, as powerful moments for the class and for me.

When Kees discusses live some of the defining moments he reviews in this book, he touches on three important, complementary domains:

There is the "business" domain, which features competitors to study, consumers and customers to understand, product lines to enrich through innovation or to prune to reduce complexity.

There is the "leadership" domain, where individuals and teams need to be energized and/or mobilized, structures need to be changed, individuals hired, developed or fired, resistance overcome.

Executives can listen to what Kees did and ask themselves what they would have done, and what they should do, under similar circumstances. This discussion leads to powerful insights on the "business" and "leadership" fronts.

But I think Kees's sessions have an even more powerful impact on the "personal" front:

• Kees's very presence in the classroom raises important questions for the audience. Here is a very successful senior executive, who decided to retire early from corporate life in order to pursue other interests in his life. Implicitly or explicitly, Kees's decision highlights to the audience that staying on is a choice! It leads participants to ask themselves, "Am I still happy doing what I do? Am I giving my time and energy to the right cause? Is this really the best use of my time?"

• Some of Kees's defining moments have also involved difficult emotions for him. Without dwelling on these emotions, Kees always acknowledges the uncertainty, the doubts and the grief he sometimes has had to come to terms with and overcome. This is very important because it helps the participants – all of whom also face such emotions, but many of whom have difficulties admitting this fact to themselves, let alone to others – to acknowledge the emotions, which is a first step towards discussing them and learning to manage them more effectively.

Kees's session has become a highlight of the Breakthrough Programme for Senior Executives, IMD's most senior "general management programme".

The title that Jean-François gave the session was simply "Defining Moments by Kees van der Graaf". The connection with the audience worked well and the feedback was surprisingly positive. Since then, I have continued to share my "defining moments" in IMD's classrooms. In fact, telling my stories have become a new passion for me. This has been fuelled by the positive feedback I have received from programme participants. On several occasions, they have asked if I had ever considered writing my stories down. It had not crossed my mind, but it inspired me to give it a try. And thanks to Jean-François, I had a title for this book. My passion for storytelling is also driven by my strong desire to help the next generation of leaders become more effective. By sharing the stories of some of the significant events in my life that have helped to shape and define me personally, professionally and spiritually, I hope to contribute to the development of the next generation. I do not pretend to know everything; the only thing I do know is that I have experienced deep learning over the years. I have made mistakes, but I have also had my successes, and I have become much more values-driven. Through this book, I would like to reach people who are interested in the heartfelt stories I have to tell and the lessons I have learnt along the way.

My one big hope is that the next generation of leaders will be more values-driven and more caring of humankind, the world, society, their loved ones and their businesses. And I believe that current leaders have an obligation to prepare and educate future leaders to put these interests above their own by spreading their knowledge, money and time to make the world a better place. I hope that I can make a small contribution to all of this by sharing my stories with you.

Throughout this book, I tell a number of stories to illustrate the points I want to make. However, there have been many more defining moments in my life – the day I married my lovely wife Renée; the birth of our three sons, each of them a different experience and all very special moments; and also the loss of my dear parents. All of these have been lasting and deeply emotional moments. They deserve a special book of their own.

Kees van der Graaf

Guide to colour-coded boxes

insights
Key insights have been highlighted throughout the book. You will find a themed summary of the insights in Chapter 5.

anecdotes
Short accounts of particular events have been included along the way to bring more life to the stories.

columnists
Friends, family and colleagues share their reflections and add their own perspectives in each of the chapters.

Introduction: The story begins

I had a very traditional Dutch upbringing. I was born in 1950 in the small city of Goes on one of the islands in the southwest of the Netherlands. My father was the director of the Zeeland branch office of De Nederlanden van 1845 insurance company when the North Sea flooded in February 1953, leaving large parts of Goes under water for nearly six months. Shortly after the flood, he was promoted to a position in the company's head office in The Hague, probably as a token of appreciation for his services during the disaster.

My family lived a very frugal lifestyle in The Hague. It was shortly after the end of World War II, and we did not have a lot of money to spend. Every week, we ate the same meals on the same days. On Thursdays, it was meatballs, Fridays, it was fish and on Sundays, bread and soup. All my school years were spent in The Hague. I had skipped the first year of primary school, so I was always one of the two or three youngest in the class. That lasted until my fourth year of secondary school when, at 14, I was just entering adolescence. Most of my classmates were 16 years old or more, rode motorbikes, smoked cigarettes and had girlfriends. I failed miserably that year, with the exception of drawing class, where I had some success. After that one setback, I had a smooth and thoroughly enjoyable finish to my secondary school years.

During my time at school, I developed a passion for sailing, thanks to my father, who took the family sailing every weekend, irrespective of the weather. There was no discussion about it. On Saturday morning when school finished at 12 noon, my mother and father would be waiting impatiently for my sister, Ineke, and me in front of the school, in their car with the engine running, so that we could go sailing.

When the time came to choose a university, I wanted to pursue my interest in drawing sailboats and become

My father – Job van der Graaf – and me

The only place I would go for a nap

Sailing with the family

a shipbuilder. My father, however, recommended that I should keep that as a hobby because there was little employment for shipbuilders. Instead, he suggested that I take generic studies related to shipbuilding to keep my options open. With that advice in mind, I chose mechanical engineering. In Holland, there are three places where you can do technical studies. Delft, the most famous, was the logical choice for all the people who lived in the western part of the Netherlands. In Eindhoven, the university was nicknamed the Philips High School. Chances were that if you went there, you would end up working for Philips for the rest of your life. Twente, the first university campus in the Netherlands, was only five years old, so everything was brand new. It was in the far east of the Netherlands, some 200 km away from home and nicely situated in the woods, between the cities of Enschede and Hengelo. At my father's suggestion, a classmate and I went for a visit, and we immediately fell in love with Twente's total approach.

In September 1968, I started my studies at Twente, and by April 1969, the Dean had summoned me to tell me that I would be better off looking for somewhere else to study. I had failed most of my exams so far! That was the wrong message for me; I was enjoying every moment of my life at Twente. So, by the following September, I was able to get myself back on track and continue with

Fellow students at Twente University

the second year. I had never realized how difficult mechanical engineering was. It took me five attempts to pass my Science of Fluids exam and eight attempts to pass Dynamics. My reputation was built around many attempts and many failures, but I was successful in the end. In 1973, I received my bachelor's degree in Mechanical Engineering. One of the unique features of Twente was that it was possible to switch from a purely technical course of study to business studies, which were designed to prepare engineers for jobs in business. So, I went on to study for my Master's in Business Engineering and celebrated my

100th exam at Twente by presenting a bottle of wine and flowers to the professor. I passed the exam before it even started, and in 1974, I completed my studies.

During my six years at Twente, I met a great group of fellow students who I lived with in a house in Enschede for the last three years of my studies. We had had enough of campus life and wanted to live in the "real world". To this day, we remain friends and spend many weeks together every year on golf and sailing holidays.

In my first year at Twente, a big gala event celebrating the university's fifth anniversary was planned. I did not have a girlfriend at the time, but I thought it would add to the enjoyment of the evening if I took a partner. My sister, Ineke, who was three years younger than me, had a very nice-looking girlfriend who lived almost next door to my parents. So, I invited my sister to the party and asked her to bring her girlfriend with her. After a lot of debate and negotiation with our parents and the other girl's parents to ease their fears about a 15-year-old schoolgirl being exposed to 18- and 19-year-old students at a party 200 km away from home, my sister and her girlfriend were allowed to come to Twente. You can imagine how grateful I am to my sister and my parents – 42 years later Renée (the girl from *almost next door*) and I are still happily married.

Renée – shortly after the gala

The last six months of my studies were spent at Hoogovens – the Dutch steel mills – developing a plan to reduce bottlenecks and increase the total capacity from 6 million to 10 million tons of steel. I loved my time there. It was the ideal place for a young mechanical and business engineer – heavy industry, down to earth, no nonsense. It was a pity that I had to leave to spend 21 months with the Dutch navy for my military service, as both parties wanted to continue the relationship.

Why I joined Unilever

The navy was great. Thanks to an attractive job as secretary of the team responsible for introducing a job evaluation system into the navy, I was given an overview of naval operations, and for the first time in my life, I was exposed to the softer side of organizations (reward, training, career path development – in short, human resources).

When the end of my navy period was in sight, I had to make a decision about my future. I talked to a few people, including my father, who made it clear to me that it was a no-brainer to stay away from consultancy and HR (which would mean continuing with the navy to do a PhD). So, I went to see Professor Jan Kreiken who had supervised my final thesis at Twente. In his very outspoken way, he concluded that none of the options I had come up with, through a process of several job interviews and hard selling, were good enough. I was

Professor Jan Kreiken

left a little speechless. So, he immediately jumped in with an alternative. I should become a product manager with Unilever! Unilever had approached him looking for candidates for the marketing function. To put it mildly, I was not impressed. Why should I join a company that puts edible fats in a tub and sells it as margarine? On top of that, Unilever was reputed to have a very tough selection process and a management team that consisted of self-important lawyers from the University of Leiden. Professor Kreiken was a real businessman – a marketer before the word marketing was invented. Among other things, he created the King Corn bread brand[1] in the Netherlands, and he was a good salesperson. He convinced me that I should go and talk to Unilever. He made a phone call, and I was scheduled to see the marketing recruiter a week later.

My perception of Unilever was that it was a dull head office, filled with boring people wearing grey three-piece suits. I arrived at Museumpark – the address of its head office in Rotterdam – on time and wearing a suit. Given that "museum" was part of the address, I was expecting the office to be full of fossils. After a long, bureaucratic process, a grim-looking guard let me in. Everything was dark – dark wood panelling and dark carpet. I was instructed to sit in an even darker, windowless corner of the lobby to wait for Mr Wolf, the marketing recruiter. Finally, he appeared, a few minutes late, adding to my already uncomfortable state. He could have been my grandfather. He was tiny, balding, with a little bit of grey hair left, and he was wearing a light grey three-piece suit. His office was dark. The architect of the building must have thought that employees should work and not be distracted by activities on the street because the windows were so high that you could not see out of them. In short, not exactly the ideal setting to convince a young engineer to join Unilever.

The first 50 minutes of the interview were as boring as I feared. But then, something unexpected happened. He

picked up the phone and called one of the Unilever operating companies in the Netherlands – Lever's Zeep Maatschappij (Lever's Detergent Company). He explained that he had just met a very interesting young man who could be a good person for Unilever. He wanted them to interview me within the next five days, introduce me to marketing and convince me it was an attractive opportunity. I was totally surprised. Behind the façade of greyness and bureaucracy, was a man of incredible action who had read me very well.

The interview at Lever's lasted a full day instead of the two hours that had originally been planned. I met all kinds of young, energetic marketing managers who were passionate about their jobs and who happened to be really nice guys. We discussed everything from the different positioning of the surface cleaners and the advertising to the reasons

why certain colours had been chosen for the labels. It was a new world for me and it was presented in a compelling way. I was hooked. I wanted to join the fascinating, dynamic world of Unilever, which surprisingly had a lot of science and technology in its products.

The roles were now reversed. Unilever had "sold" me on the benefits of joining the company, and it was now up to me to convince the company to select me. The short but tough selection process culminated in a final discussion with two senior managers for about one hour. The conversation started to go in the wrong direction when they started describing a

Calvé-de Betuwe brands

1   One of the first examples of branding a commodity in the food business in the Netherlands

Kees I did not know. I felt I had to interrupt and set them straight. Fortunately for me, that was exactly what Morris Tabaksblat and Jaap Mortier (the marketing directors of Lever's Zeep and Calvé-de Betuwe) wanted to see – Kees fighting back. An hour later, they invited me to join Unilever.

The early years at Unilever

In 1976, I began three months of sales training at Calvé-de Betuwe. As a sales representative, I was responsible for selling special offers for Calvé mayonnaise, Royco soup and de Betuwe marmalades to a series of small shops in the south of the Netherlands. One day, I unknowingly crossed the Belgian border where I was arrested for smuggling a carload of mayonnaise into the country. My name then became infamous within Unilever.

For the next five years, I worked in several different marketing jobs at Calvé-de Betuwe. After a short six-month stint in the US with Lipton Inc., I was transferred to the national personnel department as a marketing recruiter. My objective was to secure a constant stream of top talent by improving Unilever's image with students and professors. If my father had been alive, he would have fulfilled his promise of breaking my legs if I ever even considered a dead-end personnel job. He probably wouldn't have been very happy if he had seen me from his cloud in the sky, but he

Wall's Sausages

would have been comforted and pleased to know that two and a half years later I jumped straight into a senior management position with Wall's Meat in the UK.

Three years later, I moved to Frigo, Unilever's ice cream and frozen food company in Barcelona, to become the Marketing Director. It was here that I fell in love with ice cream – a fascinating product category – seasonal, fashionable and innovative – with a unique distribution model that included exclusive concessionaires (distributors) and its own freezer cabinets and kiosks.

The market was exploding. We were growing fast and expanding our factory every year. At the same time, Barcelona was preparing itself for the Olympics (described in Chapter 3). It was a delightful city in which to live with a growing family. It had good international schools and a lovely

climate. As a family, we were focused on dealing, in a positive manner, with the implications of my Unilever career. Renée had followed me wherever Unilever had asked me to go, always finding ways to enjoy herself. She did a great job of taking care of our three sons, which made it possible for me to pursue my objective of ultimately becoming the general manager of a Unilever subsidiary somewhere in the world. Our four years in Barcelona were some of our best years. We had nothing to worry about!

Bart, Michiel and Diederik

Facing consequences: Taking personal responsibility

1

After our dreamtime in Barcelona, our lives took a dramatic turn in 1992 when our oldest son Bart was diagnosed with a type of muscular dystrophy called FSHD – facio-scapulo humeral (muscular) dystrophy. As we adapted ourselves to our new circumstances, we learnt to live our lives day-to-day. And as the stories in this chapter illustrate, this event changed the course of my life. After the initial shock, social responsibility began to play a bigger role in both my personal and professional lives.

BART'S DIAGNOSIS WITH FSHD

Bart was born in December 1979. He was our first-born son, and we were so happy with his arrival. After just 20 hours in the hospital, my wife Renée and Bart were allowed to return home. My mother had already arrived to take over the household, and my father soon joined us. He was over the moon. A grandson would secure the continuation of our branch of the van der Graaf family. On top of that, Bart's second name was Job, which was also my father's name. How proud he was. He saw his new grandson

Buster Keaton [1]

a few times, but sadly, he passed away five weeks later at the age of 65. Far too young!

Bart was about six months old when Renée noticed for the first time that he was drinking and swallowing strangely. We didn't know anything about the drinking habits of newborn babies, so this phenomenon didn't concern us too much. But then, two years later, Bart was staying with Renée's sister while we were on holiday. Her husband, a general practitioner, noticed that Bart's face lacked expression. He suggested we visit a specialist.

The specialist we visited in Oxford, close to where we were living at that time, diagnosed Bart with Möbius syndrome – a disease where the nerves that steer the muscles in the face fail. The result is hardly any facial expression. The most famous example of someone with this disease is Buster Keaton, the famous film comedian. Knowing how funny Keaton was, we weren't particularly worried. Besides, we didn't find it difficult to read Bart's feelings; all we had to do was look into his eyes. Other than that, Bart was an absolutely normal kid – a fanatical and good skier and an enthusiastic football player.

By 1990, we began to see some abnormal developments in Bart's body. His

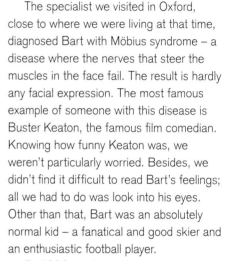

... in this chapter

- **Bart's diagnosis with FSHD**
- **Switzerland**
- **Unilever's senior executive seminar**
- **Creating the FSHD Foundation**
- **Spieren voor Spieren**
- **Reflections**

shoulder blades had begun to stand out. He also seemed to be rather slow when starting to run. So the process began of taking Bart to see a number of specialists. Specialist after specialist did not seem to know what to do about Bart's situation. We got some very different diagnoses, but none was very satisfying. So Renée and Bart went to see yet more specialists.

I had been appointed Foods Member (a terrible job title for someone who is supposed to be responsible for the food operations) in the East Asia Pacific Region. I operated out of Unilever's Rotterdam office and the regional leadership was located in the London offices. I don't know why things were set up this way; I just knew that it meant that I was constantly on the move, spending at least three weeks per month in East Asia and Australia. As a result, I was not able to be a great support for Bart and Renée. I took some consolation in enjoying the super growth in the East Asia region and designing a food strategy for that part of the Unilever world. By the time I returned home at the weekends, I was usually exhausted and not very interested in listening to more stories about different visits to different specialists. I felt like a terrible father and husband.

Kuala Lumpur, September 1992

At the end of the summer of 1992, I found myself in Kuala Lumpur for a conference I had organized for all the country leaders of our foodservice and bakery materials businesses in the region. The objective of the meeting was to agree to a roadmap for a shared approach for foodservice in the region. We set out a challenging agenda with the aim of concluding the meeting at the end of four hard days of work.

In the middle of the conference, I received an urgent phone call from the Netherlands. I left the meeting to take the call. It was Renée. She sounded very upset and was clearly in tears. She explained that she had been to see a neurologist who recognized some of Bart's symptoms. He had suggested that she take Bart to see his colleague, who specialized in a form of muscular dystrophy called FSHD. The expert confirmed that Bart had all the symptoms of FSHD.

I had no idea what FSHD was. I couldn't imagine what it meant. When I heard that FSHD was a muscular dystrophy, my first reaction was that it could be treated with physiotherapy and a muscle pain relief gel. But Renée went on to tell me everything she knew about this rare disease. FSHD is a progressive disease, meaning that the physical condition of the patient would deteriorate over time. There was no cure or therapy. There was very little known about what caused the symptoms. When I put down

What is FSHD?

The facio-scapulo humeral form of muscular dystrophy (FSHD) is a rare, hereditary form of muscular dystrophy caused by a genetic defect. It has several characteristic symptoms, like the progressive weakening, and eventually the loss of strength in the skeletal muscles. The most commonly affected muscles are facial (facio), shoulder (scapulo) and upper arm (humeral) muscles.

The progression of the disease can vary greatly, and it is hard to predict. In most cases, FSHD muscle involvement starts in the face and slowly progresses to the shoulder and upper arm muscles and then down to the abdominal and foot extensor muscles. Initial signs of FSHD include difficulty reaching above the shoulder level, foot drop, scapular winging and facial weakness. In more than half of FSHD cases, there are other symptoms including hearing loss of mainly high frequency tones. In certain cases, people suffer from vision problems. Although not typical, some people with FSHD have respiratory insufficiency, especially those with severe FSHD.

FSHD is an equal opportunity disease – anyone, regardless of age, gender, race or ethnicity, can inherit or develop it. It is the third most prevalent muscular dystrophy affecting men, women and children. It has worldwide distribution and has an incidence of 1:20,000. The disease generally presents outward signs in 95% of affected individuals by the second decade of life for men, and the third decade of life for women. In about 5% of all cases, young children are afflicted. Though FSHD is seen as a mild and benign disorder, more than 20% of patients end up using wheelchairs.

the phone, I was lost. I did not know what to do. My instincts told me to take the first flight home. My rational side reminded me that I had to bring the conference to a close. I was torn between my rational and my emotional side. After another chat with Renée, we decided that I should stay in Kuala Lumpur; there was nothing I could do for now. To this day, I still think that I should have gone home.

After talking with Renée, I headed back to the meeting. In the elevator, I bumped into Peter Polhuijs, who was a conference participant and the Chairman of Unilever Korea. He immediately noticed that there was something wrong with me, so he suggested that we leave the hotel to have a talk. After a long conversation, during which he allowed me to share my feelings with him, I had regained enough energy to continue to lead the meeting.

After the diagnosis: *Carpe diem*

When I returned to the Netherlands, we began to find out everything we could about FSHD. Renée and I both found it

East Asia & Pacific Region Foods Conference

extremely difficult to talk about it. It is such an awful feeling to know that your son has a disease and there is nothing you can do about it. We wanted to do everything we could for him to ensure he had a great and enjoyable future. But we had no idea where to start. We felt so incapable. So, because we had to do something, we joined the Dutch Muscular Dystrophy Patients'

Organization. At the very least, they could give us some information.

As the years passed and Bart's physical condition worsened, we developed a *carpe diem* attitude, whereby we focused on enjoying today, doing what we still could and worrying about any issues that might arise only as and when we were faced with them.

SWITZERLAND: MY FIRST CEO ROLE

After three years as the Foods Member of the East Asia Pacific Regional Management Group, I was offered my first Chairmanship of an operating company – Lipton Sais in Zurich – by the President of the Southern European Region. Lipton Sais had quite an unusual portfolio of activities, which included an oil mill, an oil refinery and a margarine factory. Lipton Sais also had a large herb and spice business under the brand name Butty, which it sold through the retail channel to the final consumer and via the foodservice channel to hotels, restaurants and institutions. The company made these products in a small factory near Lausanne together with a large volume of Lipton Tea products.

Additionally, the company owned Betty Bossi – a publishing company. In the 1960s and 1970s, Betty Bossi, evolved from publishing a series of recipe leaflets for margarine-based cooking and baking to publishing a cooking magazine. It had 975,000 subscriptions in Switzerland. With a population of four to five million, this meant that almost every Swiss household subscribed to Betty Bossi. It was so popular and its recipes were so well liked that you could count on getting the same meal served several times over when you dined with friends and colleagues during the Christmas holiday season. I remember receiving a call from Migros (one of the two largest retailers in Switzerland) one day in December asking me to warn them in advance about the Betty Bossi Christmas menu suggestions so that they could anticipate what ingredients to stock up on. The previous year, the dinner menu included tiramisu as a dessert and there was such an explosive demand for mascarpone that Migros ran out of stock within a few days. If they had known the menu in advance, they could have stocked up on mascarpone and sold a lot more.

Next to the successful magazine, Betty Bossi ran a successful cookery school, had a large side business that sold a small selection of cookery utensils and kitchenware and published three to four cookbooks per year. Most of the cookbooks topped the list of bestselling books sold in Switzerland for many months. It was a lovely, highly profitable business, which provided Lipton Sais with millions of Swiss francs in working capital every December when the subscriptions were paid. It had its own Managing Director, who reported to me. However, the Chief Editor, a rather independent and difficult person to manage, had completely lost the notion that Betty Bossi was part of Unilever Switzerland, which meant it was obliged to promote Lipton Sais products. Some recipes even used butter instead of Unilever margarine. This was like swearing in church to a through-and-through Unilever man. But the editor continued to claim her editorial freedom. Lipton Sais was indeed a rather unique member of the Unilever family. It was in a unique country with all kind of protectionist measures, duties and levies.

Charles Miller Smith, the Unilever Board member responsible for the Europe-South region, briefed me in his particular style – short, friendly and clear, very clear. "Kees", he said, "go to Switzerland for three years and sort this portfolio out for me. Sell Betty Bossi, sell the herb and spice business, get rid of the oil mill and the refinery, acquire 100% of the shares or get rid of Margo (the Swiss bakery business) and turn Lipton Sais into a real fast-moving consumer goods company with a decent profit. You have one year to understand the business, one year to implement what I just said and one year to enjoy the skiing". It all sounded pretty demanding to me, but it also seemed logical. Plus, the prospect of some skiing – one of my favourite sports – was attractive. He informed me that Unilever's offices would be moved from Zurich to Zug in a year or two for cost and tax reasons. He also mentioned that he planned to come to Switzerland in the spring for a long weekend. Thursday and Friday we would work in the office, Friday evening we would drive to Gstaad, where we would discuss business and life (or life and business) in a nice setting. During the day, we would do some skiing, and in the evening go for a sauna and some good food. This indeed happened. I found it initially rather strange, but in hindsight, it was a super idea.

In four days, we had designed and agreed on a master plan. He gave me his trust and the confidence to implement it. I felt fully supported, empowered and therefore responsible.

Moving the family

Before I knew about the opportunity in Switzerland, I started to prepare my family for a move away from Wassenaar, where our home was based in the Netherlands. One evening, I asked the boys over supper what they thought about the idea of going back to Spain. As mentioned, we loved our time there; it had been our favourite country so far. If I was offered a senior position there, I said that I wouldn't hesitate to accept it without a discussion at home. This was met with very little response.

After dinner, the boys went upstairs to go to bed. The next morning at breakfast, Bart, being the oldest, started the discussion. "Dad", he said, "last night you mentioned the idea of going back to Spain. We discussed it upstairs and we have a different opinion. If it is really necessary to go abroad again we do not want to go to Spain. We would rather go to a new country". I was really surprised. Positively surprised. Because in one sentence, he delivered some big messages: 1) moving again is not our first wish; 2) if it is necessary, we want to have a new experience. Great!

A few months later Charles offered me the Swiss Chairmanship. We all knew

The saga of selling Betty Bossi

Unilever had dollar signs in its eyes when it started to think about the possible profits from disposing of Betty Bossi. A bank was appointed to act in the disposal process. It convincingly confirmed the likelihood of getting more than CHF100 million (significantly more than two times sales). It invited many prospective buyers to participate in the auction process. All three large publishing companies in Switzerland participated. One evening, I read in the newspaper that the CEOs of these companies had met each other at a party in a large hotel in the centre of Zurich. The journalist reported that the three CEOs surprisingly disappeared into a private room. At that time, it was a meaningless piece of news for me. However, a few weeks later, we received the Non-Binding Indication of Value (NBIV) of all bidders. The three Swiss bids were within CHF500,000 of each other, and all were far too low, but slightly above another competing buyer. Of course, the two situations had nothing to do with each other!

In the meantime, I strongly suspected that the information I was sharing on a weekly basis with the Betty Bossi management team was being leaked to the Swiss market. Rather than confront the issue, I took advantage of it when an ideal opportunity presented itself. Barings approached us about a management buy-out (MBO). It was prepared to pay twice the amount of the Swiss publishers. I shared this information with the Betty Bossi team and made it very clear to them that I loved the idea. On top of that, it would make the management team very rich over time. Within

days, I was invited by Ringier, the highest bidder of the Swiss publishing companies to come to their offices to discuss Betty Bossi. I informed the bank and asked for someone to attend the meeting, but due to a conflict with another meeting, this was not possible. On top of that, it was the bank's opinion that it would be purely an exploratory meeting.

I had become so suspicious in those days, that I always had my files with me in a sealed briefcase. Holding the briefcase close to my chest, I walked through the parking garage of Ringier and on to the meeting room. To my surprise, six people were facing me when I entered the room. After a round of friendly greetings, it became apparent that they wanted to close the deal. I explained that I had the Barings offer that was valued at twice their offer. At a certain moment, after lengthy arguments from the Ringier side that the Barings offer was ridiculous, I instinctively wrote down a number – the price at which I would agree to sell – on a small piece of paper. I folded it, shoved it towards the CEO and said, "This is the price, take it or leave it." The meeting was stopped. I left the room. After 45 minutes, I was called back in. The CEO shook my hand and said, "You have a deal."

They structured it in such a way that it was also attractive from a tax point of view. I called Charles Miller Smith who was over the moon. I also called the people at the bank. They had not realized that the moment to strike a deal was so close. They were shocked and embarrassed.

Switzerland from our Christmas skiing holidays. We loved those weeks together on the slopes. Imagine being able to ski every weekend. This would be fabulous. How different it would be.

Just before Christmas, Renée and I went house hunting. We knew all the tricks. First, we selected the school. The prospect of Unilever's offices moving from Zurich to Zug, made us choose Institut Montana, a semi-boarding school on a hill above Zug. It had a good reputation and our children did not have to become boarders. As a result, we looked for a house close to the school. We found a magnificent villa just above the village of Ober Aegeri – a 10-minute drive from the office and a 15-minute drive from the school. I would be able to drop the boys off at school before going to the office.

Because of the school system, I went to Switzerland alone in December. At the weekends, I went home to Wassenaar. In June, at the end of the school year, the family moved to Ober Aegeri. We enjoyed the summer and settled in reasonably smoothly. Once school started, the children had to get used to the students that boarded at the school. Often, they were the children of very rich parents. Some of them were literally dropped off at the school not knowing that they would not see their parents for a year. Their pocket money was sometimes more than a small salary! So much for the nouveaux riches and their family values.

In December, the first snow came, and Renée took the children to a nearby ski resort on a free afternoon from school. There, she learnt the hard way that Bart's physical strength had deteriorated. He could not take the ski lift by himself, he

> **insight**
>
> *Show genuine interest in your managers' family situations. Be creative in offering small gestures with big impact. The loyalty gains will be enormous.*

could not get back on his feet again after a fall and his ski boots were too heavy for him to walk. This was the last time he ever skied. For all of us, and most of all for Bart, this was a big emotional moment – it was so unfair. There he was in Switzerland, the dream location for his favourite sport, and he discovered that it was over for him. He dealt with it in a very mature way. But still, I wondered what was going on in his mind – anger, disappointment, sadness.

We quickly learnt that Switzerland has one big problem. It is not flat. You have to go either uphill or downhill to get anywhere. And that was not compatible with a muscular dystrophy problem. Bart could not easily walk from one school building to another or take a bike to go visit a friend. His mother became his private driver, taking him all around so that he would not end up socially isolated. In the winter, this sometimes meant putting snow chains on several times per day – in the morning to

get down the mountain from our house, taking them off at the bottom and then putting them on again to climb up to the school. The same ritual had to be repeated three more times. Needless to say, Renée became a real expert at putting on and taking off snow chains. This was no quality of life for Bart and Renée. Eventually, we all reached the conclusion that the family had to move back to Holland.

We decided to inform Unilever that we would move back to Holland at the end of the school year and that I would take an apartment in Zug, and continue as Chairman of Lipton Sais. I first talked to Jan Peelen. He had been my boss in East Asia Pacific and was now the Unilever HR Director on the board. Charles Miller Smith had been succeeded by Okko Mueller, who I informed after I got the OK from Jan Peelen. All agreed that the family would repatriate and that I would stay in Zug.

Behind the scenes, however, something else was going on. Jan Peelen and Antony Burgmans, (respectively, at the time, Unilever's Chief HR Officer and President of Europe – see Appendix II, 1993–1995) had decided that this was not the right solution. Unilever has a deep-rooted belief that families should not be apart; they should be together abroad, supporting each other. Otherwise, it could become a recipe for disaster. Somewhere around Easter, Antony invited me to come and see him in Rotterdam. It had worked out that the current product group executive of the ice cream category had decided to leave Unilever to become the managing director of Südzucher. Südzucher owned Schöller, which was a direct competitor of Unilever with its Mövenpick and Schöller ice cream ranges. Unilever was furious about such an act of unethical behaviour and had asked the executive to leave the premises immediately. It also wanted a

Bart's Column

Just Dad to me

Bart van der Graaf

It was sometimes difficult to be confronted with my father's book. Not only does he write about his work for Unilever but he also writes about our family. He discusses some difficult periods that we as a family have had to endure – the moment I was diagnosed with FSHD, the day I was no longer able to ski, the time we were forced to leave Switzerland and return to Wassenaar because of my illness. As I read his book, I experienced these moments again. That was difficult.

But, above all, I am proud of my father. His book shows that he continues to do so much to fight FSHD. It is possible for a father to react passively when his son is diagnosed with a condition like FSHD. But he never did. He set up the FSHD Foundation, and the income from his lectures go to the Foundation. I find it very special that he continues to spend so much time and energy on this project.

His book is about finding a balance in life. I think he became aware of what he wanted from life when he spent some time alone on a mountain. He decided to leave Unilever and become more involved with society and have more time for his family. I am sure that he has found the right balance, and we as a family are very happy about that. He is now much more relaxed when he is with us. In the past, he was rather stressed on the first few days of a holiday. Work was probably very much on his mind. Now he is chilled out right from the beginning!

He has not always been an easygoing father. Sometimes he was inclined to try to force his will on us. For example, he once absolutely insisted that we should take the car to our holiday home in Marbella. "We have to take the car so that we can take the tool kit with us." This was his argument! The rest of the family wanted to fly instead of spending three days in the car. Fortunately, we were eventually able to persuade him that driving was not a good idea. It took some time but in the end he agreed.

In this book, he describes how to reduce complexity within a company and how to inspire staff to commit to a project. He explains how, through optimum communication, it is possible to get everyone thinking and working towards one goal. If colleagues disagreed with him, he remained true to his vision and tried to convince them. This usually worked because he is good at solving problems and is able to inspire others. The lessons in his book are very educational. I have experienced some of the same situations at work that he describes. Now that I know how to solve these problems, it will only be a matter of time before I become the new CEO of CSM!

At my father's farewell symposium, many Unilever colleagues praised him highly. They said that they had learned so much from him and that he was such a good boss. It was very special to hear this sort of praise, because for me he's just Dad. And now, he has written a life story – a personal, inspiring and sometimes spiritual tale. It is clear that he has always been there for us and always will be. For this reason, I am very proud of him.

quick replacement to show the rest of Unilever that it could act very fast when such an unacceptable move was made by an employee. Lucky me.

I was offered the job and became the ultimate brand custodian responsible for the global strategy of the ice cream business. It was a dream job, located in Rotterdam, with strong ties to the European Ice Cream and Frozen Foods business group that was led by Antony Burgmans. As one can imagine, I did not have to think twice. The family would be together again in the Netherlands, and I would have the job of a lifetime. Because I had to start in early May, and the children had to finish their school year, I moved back to the Netherlands two months ahead of the family. Our house was not yet available, so my mother asked me to stay with her. This was a special experience – being mothered at the age of 45 for a couple of months. My mother loved it, and I got spoiled. Every day, she would ask if I had my passport, my money and my driver's license with me. I had forgotten all about that special feature of a mother caring for her son.

A unique mother

My mother deserves a special mention given what she has done for the family. She taught us the real meaning of life, the importance of values and she kept the family together, by who she was. Always interested, always present, following my sister's family and my family, wherever we were sent by our employers. She showed up in Brazil, Singapore, Taiwan, US, UK and Spain, irrespective of her age. She became the grandmother who was universally adored by all her grandchildren because of her uncomplicated, authentic way of showing love and care. She was funny, outspoken, direct and non-political.

She loved football and used strong language when watching football matches. She supported different teams – Feyenoord, PSV or Ajax – depending on which grandchildren she was visiting. A beautiful moment was when I took her, at the age of 85, with my family to the Holland vs. Scotland football match in the Arena near Amsterdam. It was the first time she had ever attended a match in a stadium. Holland won 5-0. She behaved like a hooligan, and had the evening of a lifetime, leaving her grandsons astonished.

She nursed all of our children as well as those of my little sister. As soon as we announced that Renée was in labour and that it was time to go to the hospital, she would appear and take over the household for at least a week.

She was the embodiment of family values, constantly stressing the importance of a good family and why it is essential to invest in nurturing the family ties.

UNILEVER'S SENIOR EXECUTIVE SEMINAR – 1995

In 1995, Unilcvcr brought together a group of 25 senior leaders from across the organization and from all parts of the world. All were classified as "high potential" or "board material". Clive Butler, one of Unilever's Board members, was the content leader for this seminar. The programme was two weeks long with three months in between each week during which we had to go into the field and visit so-called excellent, best practice organizations. Professor C.K. Prahalad (C.K.), the late management expert and business philosopher, was asked to lead the group and teach us how to compete on foresight.

The group gathered at Four Acres, Unilever's training centre in Kingston upon Thames, UK.

For those who did not know C.K., I can share with you that he was someone who was not only very bright, but also very inspiring, challenging and out of the ordinary; it was a real privilege to have spent two full weeks in the company of such a special person.

The objective of the senior executive seminar (SES) was to identify the long-term, future growth areas for Unilever in terms of territories, categories and R&D. It was a difficult task. We had to present the findings at the end of the SES

to both Chairmen, Morris Tabaksblat and Niall FitzGerald.

At that time, I was still struggling with the question, "What should I do to help Bart?" I had contemplated alternatives, such as resigning from Unilever and studying medicine to become a specialist in FSHD. This was not a realistic option as I could not and cannot see myself cutting into human beings or giving injections.

C.K. gave me the big idea

One day during the programme, C.K. was in front of the class passionately arguing that one should always set very ambitious targets. He was not talking about targets for bonus purposes, but about visionary targets – things you dream of. His argument was very powerful. He stated that if you aim high, and if you put all your energy behind meeting your target, you will be surprised by how far you can go. You will certainly go much further than you would if you had aimed for the traditional "ambitious, but realistic target".

He illustrated his point with the example of the high jump. Top performing athletes always try to break world records. While

Unilever's Four Acres Training Centre

From the scissors technique ... [2]

... to breaking records with the Fosbury Flop

applying the traditional scissors technique, progress was slow for many years. It seemed physically impossible to jump any higher. Then, Dick Fosbury developed the *Fosbury Flop* and all of a sudden, records were being broken again.

While C.K. was sharing this example with the classroom, my thoughts went back to Bart and FSHD. I was wondering if there was something in what C.K. had just said that I could apply to our family situation. What did "aiming high" mean for FSHD? The aim had to be "a cure for FSHD". EUREKA! I could contribute to achieving

that goal by raising large amounts of money to make it possible for scientists to understand what causes FSHD and develop adequate therapies. Creating a foundation seemed to be a great idea. But it had to be a different kind of foundation – one without overheads and one that would spend the money rather than accumulating a lot of wealth. It also had to be one that would not ask the scientists to write 20-page research proposals; instead, it would look for short, convincing arguments so that it could make quick decisions, rather than taking months and months

to evaluate proposals before deciding. It would bring the scientists together and get them to agree on a common research strategy for FSHD.

> ## insight
>
> *... The moral of this story is that if, you want to break new ground and set new standards, you have to rethink your models, your way of doing things. You have to be brave, and you have to have the courage to do things differently, leaving old conventions behind.*

CREATING THE FSHD FOUNDATION

In the following months, I went to see as many specialists, medical doctors and experts in the field of genetics as possible, to find out if more money was needed to fund research into FSHD. One other large organization in the Netherlands – the Princess Beatrix Fund – was financially supporting research in the field of muscular dystrophy. However, since the funds were being allocated to all the 350 different forms of muscular dystrophy, the amount available for FSHD was limited. I also met Elisabeth Vroom, President of the Duchenne Parents Project. Duchenne is the most prevalent of muscular dystrophies, and it generally afflicts only males. It is characterized by the degeneration of the heart and lung muscles, which results in a shortened life expectancy for those afflicted. This foundation was very similar to the one I wanted to create – fast, pragmatic, no-nonsense, unconventional and passionately led by Elisabeth – a great model to follow.

The pharmaceutical industry, as I discovered, is not very interested in funding basic research into rare diseases – the low occurrence rate makes it economically uninteresting. It only gets interested when researchers have discovered the root cause of the disease and are ready to test the therapy in a large-scale clinical trial.

It was not at all difficult to find people willing to join the board of the Foundation.

Every single person I approached accepted my invitation, which drove home the importance of a good network of friends. I had a nice mix of people with expertise in the fields of organizing events, medicine in general and FSHD in particular, research, finance and fundraising.

> **insight**
>
> *... fast, pragmatic, no-nonsense, unconventional and passionately led ... a great model to follow.*

The launch of the FSHD Foundation

In order to demonstrate that the foundation was a reliable and trustworthy organization, I needed to establish a "VIP" committee that could recommend the Foundation. Here again, I must have been very convincing, and most likely very passionate, because everybody I asked – from Morris Tabaksblat to Professor Galjaard and Johan Cruijff (the retired Dutch footballer) – was happy to join the committee.

I also needed money to get started. Of course, I provided initial funding myself as did quite a number of my friends, family members and colleagues from Unilever. On June 27, 1997, Renée and I went to see the notary to formalize the creation of the FSHD Stichting (Foundation). At 4 pm, we were sitting in the notary's office, ready to sign the documents. I gave Renée the

> **insight**
>
> *Never underestimate the importance of a good network of real friends ... if you look after them, they will always be there, ready to support you, when you need them.*

pen so she could sign first. At that exact moment, lightning flashed and thunder roared. We both saw this as a good sign and were even more confident that we were doing the right thing.

That evening, we had a garden party for all the people that had joined the board and the committees, including some other guests from the Universities in Leiden and Nijmegen, where FSHD research was concentrated. I remember telling my children in my speech that they should nurture their friendships because, as they could see, four of my classmates from my final year at school were present that evening and they were involved in the newly created FSHD Stichting. The five of us were ready to support each other whenever necessary – a compelling example of real friendship.

The FSHD Foundation's first year

Very quickly, I learnt how difficult it is to get such an organization off the ground. It requires a lot of hard work. But we enjoyed it. Another important benefit was that Renée and I learnt to talk about FSHD and our son's condition without getting

The Foundation as a partner in FSHD research

LUMC FSHD research team

Silvère van der Maarel

Professor, Leiden University Medical Center
www.lumc.nl

For decades, Dutch researchers have played a prominent role in researching the cause and treatment of FSHD. The study was initiated at the end of the 1980s by Professors Frants and Padberg who began searching for the genetic defect that caused FSHD. Now, more than 20 years later, we know much more about FSHD and we have a reliable diagnosis. As a result, our efforts are now focused on how we can best treat people with FSHD.

Why has the Netherlands played such a prominent international role in leading the research in this area for more than two decades? There are several reasons. Besides the ambition and affinity of the founders and their successors for the FSHD research program, this has largely been determined by the research infrastructure – good cooperation between the physicians and the basic scientists, close contact with patients and patient organizations, a good health care system and a solid basis of funding for the research.

The FSHD Foundation plays a unique role in this respect. Since its inception in 1997, it has been closely involved in FSHD research in the Netherlands and abroad, and it gives direction to new research through its "Roadmap to Solutions". It also facilitates pilot projects by leveraging sufficient funds from NWO, the EU and other organizations that fund scientific research. Finally, it contributes significantly to the continuity of research in the Netherlands wherever necessary. The FSHD Foundation, therefore, plays a unique and indispensible role in the Dutch research field. Now that the research is gaining momentum, I look forward to continuing to work with the FSHD Foundation.

LEIDS UNIVERSITAIR MEDISCH CENTRUM

Sculpture by Marte Röling

too emotional. Emotion became passion. It took the pressure off our relationship. The frustrated energy we suppressed in the past had now found a channel for release. (See Appendix III for the FSHD Foundation: Roadmap to Solutions – Strategy 2008–2011.)

Unilever's support was impressive. On one occasion, it even organized an auction to sell part of its art collection in support of the Foundation. It organized an event around the opening of an exhibition of young, promising artists. Many Unilever and

non-Unilever guests were in attendance.

The auctioneer from Christie's did a marvellous job of generating a fantastic result for the Foundation. There was one item, a specially created "sculpture" by Marte Röling, that did not reach its target. I decided to take it out of the auction and I am still hoping to find a company that is prepared to become the proud owner of this piece of art for the sum of €25,000.

I was again aware of the importance of a large network. The more people you know, the greater the chances are that there will be individuals willing to support you in realizing your goals. If they cannot help directly, they are often able to put you in contact with others who can. As a consequence, I started to work even harder to keep my career at Unilever progressing; it was clear to me that the higher I was able to go, the more I would be able to benefit the Foundation through my network. As I started to discover the power of the relationship between my job and my work in society, I subconsciously started to develop my three-circle model (see Preface).

Reanimated "junk" genes are found to cause disease[3]

The above headline appeared in the *International Herald Tribune* on Saturday-Sunday, August 21-22, 2010. The human genome is riddled with dead genes, fossils of a sort, dating back hundreds of thousands of years. Scientists were surprised when they discovered that these dead genes can rise from the dead and cause one of the most common forms of muscular dystrophy – FSHD. It is the first time geneticists have seen a dead gene come back to life and cause a disease. According to Dr Francis Collins, "If we were thinking of a collection of the genome's greatest hits, this would go on the list."

Previously, the cause of FSHD was poorly understood. The work has revealed a way to search for treatments.

This breakthrough is thanks in part to the FSHD Foundation. According to Professor Silvère van der Maarel, "The FSHD Foundation is always prepared to support pilot studies, which means that our team can continue with this important research project."

SPIEREN VOOR SPIEREN (MUSCLES FOR MUSCLES)

In September 1997, a visitor came to my office in Rotterdam. He explained that he had called Johan Cruijff with the wild idea of doing fundraising for muscular dystrophy. Johan had immediately referred him to me, telling him that if he wanted to organize something for muscle diseases, I was the person to talk to because "Kees knows everything about muscle diseases".

The visitor spoke for half an hour. At times, I had no idea what he was talking about. When he finally stopped, I asked him a few questions to get a feel for what he wanted.

A robot arm for Bas Pistoor

My understanding was that he wanted to bring together a number of "football VIPs" to raise sufficient money for a robot arm for a young boy that suffered from Duchenne muscular dystrophy. At that time (1996), boys who had Duchenne muscular dystrophy were barely expected to reach the age of 16 or 18 because the disease also affected the heart and lung muscles.

The boy's name was Bas Pistoor. He had a good wheelchair, but he could not use his arms any longer. He had to be washed, dressed and fed. A robot arm, directed with a joystick, would make it possible for him to do many things by himself again. But the instrument would cost well over €50,000.

The idea was to organize a rock concert on the third day of Christmas to raise money for the robot arm. The lead donors were the de Boer brothers (Frank and Ronald, both from AJAX), Jan Reker (President of the Football Coaches Association) and Rob Cohen (Ronald de Boer's father-in-law and the director of Team Holland).

The Johan Cruijff Golf Tournament

A year earlier, thanks to the Spanish branch of Ogilvy & Mather, Bart, Renée and I were invited to a golf tournament organized by Johan Cruijff. It was at the famous La Peralada golf course in the north of Spain, and many football celebrities (players and coaches) participated. They were teamed up with people who were prepared to pay a fortune for the privilege of spending a day golfing with their heroes. The revenues went to Johan's foundation – the Johan Cruijff Welfare Foundation.

After a practice round, we went via our hotel to the castle where the gala dinner was to take place. Upon arrival, Johan immediately welcomed us as his "special guests". We felt honoured. The place was packed with football celebrities. Bart (aged 17 at the time) was impressed, and so was I. We were seated at a table with Marco van Basten, Guus Hiddink and an Italian football friend of Marco's. It was a smashing evening. At the end of it, there was a lottery and the grand prize was the shirt that Marco van Basten wore during his last official football match for AC Milan. And the winner was of course Bart! Marco signed it for him.

Later, I was told that Martin Jol, the previous trainer/coach of AJAX in 2009 and 2010, claimed to have the real shirt and that he refused to give it to the AJAX Museum. In order to find out which one is authentic, we would probably have to do a sweat test!

During the tournament, Renée and I played with John Toshak, a former football coach for several clubs, including Real Madrid in the 1990s. He was a real coach. He could make you do things you did not realise you could do. He consistently called me Kaas (which means cheese in Dutch) instead of Kees. Bart nearly had a heart attack from laughing so hard. At one point, I was hesitating over what club to use. It was on a par 5 with a 190-meter tree-lined, narrow corridor to go before reaching the centre of the green. He came to me, put his arm around my shoulder and said, "Kaas (cheese), what is the distance?" "190 meters," I said. "What club do you need for that distance?" "A 3 wood," was my answer. "OK, then take your 3 wood." I attempted to point out how narrow the entrance to the green was. No chance. Toshak wasn't taking any excuses, "If we want to win, we have to get a 3 here, because you already have 2 strokes on this hole." And when the coach says do it, you do it! Total concentration, head down, think positively, steady swing and BANG. A perfect shot, that landed just before the green then rolled on to it.

The lesson – concentrate and go for it. After a great day of golf, we returned home, an experience and a great shirt richer.

Involving the Dutch National Football Team

The first time I met Jan Reker and Rob Cohen, they had started to toy with the idea of involving the Dutch National Football team, which had qualified for the World Cup tournament in France in 1998.

Jan's Column

Born lucky

Jan Reker
Former Technical Director of PSV Eindhoven
Member, Spieren voor Spieren (Muscles for Muscles) Board

Being a trainer and a coach is fantastic. It is second best only to being a pro football player. Trainers, often former pros, are adults, while footballers are young and have little life experience. In general, top sports people are highly individualistic. Their life revolves around how they perform, and everything else is in second place. Young sports people who are building their careers pay almost no attention to anything else. In football, this is taken to the extreme. Players live in a world in which everything is taken care of for them; they earn more than their contemporaries do and they are often hugely popular. They have no idea how exceptional their position is. They don't realize that it is thanks to the talents they were born with that their future is so bright.

As a coach, you want to convince your players of just how lucky they are to have been born with so much talent. You want them to be motivated to do anything for it. Telling them that some children are born with a disability instead of with special talents is very confrontational. There's you, the player who was born with talent, and there's your neighbour, a boy or girl with a hereditary muscle disease. It happened to you, it happened to them, and neither of you had anything to say about it. And so all these lucky young people with their aptitude for sports need to help their contemporaries who were less lucky with the bodies they got. The healthy muscles working to care for the ones that are sick.

Wouldn't it be great to organize a "farewell and success" type of event, get it televised and raise a lot of money for children with muscular dystrophy?

I volunteered to think about a possible set-up. A few months earlier, I had completed the establishment of my own FSHD Foundation. I had the experience, and the do's and don'ts were still fresh in my mind.

Over a simple Indonesian meal in the canteen of the tennis hall where the concert would take place a few hours later, I presented the plans to create another foundation, with a board consisting of all the people involved in the robot arm event: Jan Reker, Gerard Pijl, Ton Smits, Woody Louwerens, Rob Cohen, Ronnie Gerstanovich (the director of the Princess Beatrix Fund) and myself. They liked the plans so much that I was asked to chair the board and to start work on creating the Foundation called "Spieren voor Spieren" – "Muscles for Muscles" – healthy muscles in support of people with sick muscles.

By January 1998, we existed – five months after the stranger came to my office. And then the real work began. We needed to find answers to simple questions like:

- How do we get the Dutch football team players enthusiastic?
- How do we get the Dutch Football Association (KNVB) on board?
- How do we convince the official sponsors of the KNVB to embrace our idea and to contribute €220,000?
- How do we select a good production company, with a great presenter?
- How do we develop a programme format that can generate millions?
- Which network would be prepared to give us three hours of their TV time?

The Heartbrand[4] launch

When Spieren voor Spieren being launched, I was Product Group Executive for the global ice-cream category. We had made the brave decision to move to one heart-shaped logo worldwide that would be applied to all brands in the ice-cream operations – Ola, Wall's, Frigo, Lusso, Algida, etc. The team had worked very hard to convince most stakeholders that this was the correct move.

Both Board members – Lex Kemner and Antony Burgmans – were very much in favour of the logo. Unfortunately, one of the Unilever Chairmen, during a visit to East Asia, was confronted by a number of Company Chairmen who were lobbying against the new logo. The CFO of Unilever was also dead set against it.

An extraordinary board meeting was called to discuss the matter. This was highly unusual for such a small matter. Marlies Ponsioen, the ice-cream advertising member and I had to do the presentation. We rehearsed and rehearsed. We also decided that we would resign if the Board rejected the change.

The atmosphere in the boardroom was quite tense. The Chairman opened the meeting and after a short introduction gave the floor to me. I began explaining the reasons for the change, which were supported by convincing market research findings. After some challenges and some really critical, almost personal, attacks it was time for a decision. The support of many of the Board members was evident from their body language and even some little kicks under the table, and this spurred us on to do an outstanding job arguing in favour of the change. The Chairman concluded that there was a clear majority in favour of the new logo, and Lex Kemner and the team were thanked for the presentation of a convincing case.

Not everyone was happy, and we were not invited for lunch with the Board, which was a blessing because I was due at the Amstel Hotel in an hour for the Spieren voor Spieren lunch!

It looked impossible to deal with all these issues, particularly when we took into account the fact that we had to be on the air by the end of May 1998. Time was extremely tight.

Lunch at the Amstel Hotel

Rob Cohen had come up with a brilliant idea to help us answer all the difficult questions we were facing. He convinced Frank de Boer, the captain of the Dutch football team, Edwin van der Sar (the goalie and a very important person on the team) and Ronald de Boer to invite all the sponsors, the key people on the board of the KNVB, representatives of Team Holland (the organization that owned, although it was disputed at the time, all the portrait rights of the players of the national football team), the selected production company leader and the members of Spieren voor Spieren for a lunch at the Amstel Hotel in Amsterdam. The Amstel Hotel is arguably the most prestigious hotel in the Netherlands, and certainly not cheap. At that point, we had an empty bank account.

To my surprise, but not to Rob Cohen's, everybody showed up. One has to realize that at that time, the parties involved were all having problems with each other:
- The sponsors were unhappy with what they were getting for their money.
- The KNVB did not like the role that Team Holland was playing.
- There were tensions between certain groups of players on the national team.
- Team Holland wanted a lot of money for the portrait rights.

Maybe they all came because they were hoping that Spieren voor Spieren could become the glue that would repair the many broken relationships.

We were all seated at a large table. Frank de Boer opened the meeting, welcomed all the guests and explained that the objective was to reach an agreement with all parties to organize a televised fundraising event with the support of the entire Dutch football team, the KNVB and its sponsors for the benefit of Spieren voor Spieren.

During lunch, there were presentations from the production company about the possible programme format and the Princess Beatrix Fund explaining the need for more scientific research in muscle diseases. I arrived from the Unilever Board meeting just in time to make the final speech. I asked for full support of the idea

The Amstel Hotel, Amsterdam

and for cash contributions of €220,000 from the sponsors, €25,000 from the KNVB and €25,000 from the players. I also asked for a guarantee of another €250,000 in case it was needed. There was a short discussion behind closed doors while we waited in the foyer. In the end, they gave us everything we had asked for except the guarantee of an additional €250,000.

Three months of extremely hard work followed. At the very last moment, we had to switch to another production company. The commercial network of the original production company was trying to get access to the players, through our organization, for other programmes – a clear example of vested interest. We found another company – the public network TROS – and got the very best presenter for this kind of fundraising event – Ivo Niehe.

The television show

For the event at the end of May 1998, we had invited many VIPs, Ministers, football authorities, families and other potential funders. I was extremely nervous. I had no official role in the programme. I only had to thank everybody after the cameras stopped recording. But I knew that we had to be successful because we had started with an overdraft in our bank account of between €250,000 and €300,000.

All the signs were positive. We got a lot of publicity in the newspapers and on the radio. People knew that something great was about to happen. We drew a very large

Michiel and FSHD

Recently, I was pleasantly surprised by a request from our youngest son Michiel. He is in the final year of his studies at the HES in Amsterdam to get his bachelor's degree in marketing. As part of the last semester of his program, he has to perform a market research project for a company or organization. I expected him to try to do this for a large organization. Instead, he approached me and asked if he could do a project for the FSHD Stichting. He wanted to explore new avenues for fundraising for a small organization in the context of the current economic crisis. Where could the FSHD Stichting get new funds for new research projects? His idea was to brainstorm a few really new ideas and test them out with industry. I was really touched by this idea. For me, it was a beautiful sign of his care for his brother and his appreciation of the work of the Foundation. He was showing his heart.

audience. People responded well to the call for donations and to register as supporters of Spieren voor Spieren. Everything seemed to be working. Seeing the players with patients was awakening the right emotions among the audience. The call centre could not cope with all the callers (despite its huge capacity). The presenter eventually had to ask potential donors to stop calling.

Behind the scenes, it was reported that some 60,000 supporters had signed in, which meant that the first NLG 2 million (about €1 million) was in the kitty. Emotions in the studio were mounting.

When the cameras stopped, it was my turn to address the audience. I gave it my best shot. My voice was shaking with emotion and I had tears in my eyes. Who could have dreamt a year ago, that all of this would become a reality? The moment I stopped talking, my youngest son, Michiel, rushed forward, jumped into my arms and gave me a very big and meaningful hug.

Later, Guus Hiddink showed that he is actually a really nice guy with a big heart. He confessed that the evening was exactly what he needed to bring the team together. We had given the Dutch national football team a real purpose. Unfortunately, they were beaten in the quarterfinals by Brazil.

KPN became the main sponsor

The following morning, I learnt why the call centre was not able to handle the large volume of incoming calls – the telephone network had collapsed because of a faulty

connection on the network. Immediately, I called our lawyer. He recommended that we hold all supplying parties accountable and that we inform the responsible Minister. Within 24 hours, we had settled with KPN, the Dutch telecom company. A good relationship was established. Maybe this laid the foundation for KPM becoming a major sponsor of Spieren voor Spieren a few years later.

The great thing about the KPN sponsorship was that the board encouraged all its employees to personally help Spieren voor Spieren and the company facilitated this. It involved the Staff Social Committee and asked them to coordinate the activities. A main KPN board member was assigned to become the contact person for the Spieren voor Spieren Board. The KPN employees were involved in a variety of activities, including:

- Dance marathons
- Volunteering to staff the call centre during subsequent television shows
- Donating the value of their Christmas parcels
- Helping children with the disease, e.g. taking them out to the countryside.

Just before Christmas 2000, I was invited to KPN's headquarters to attend a meeting with all employees. The Chairman of the Board of the Staff Social Committee presented me with a cheque for €200,000 that had been generated over the last 12 months by KPN's employees.

KPN's Board was present on this

occasion and encouraged the employees to continue with these initiatives. They made it clear that they fully supported the objectives of Spieren voor Spieren and that a large number of employees were engaged in the activities. There were also many mentions of how these activities had created a better atmosphere in the workplace.

How Unilever showed its heart

Back in 1998, after the success of the first event, we decided to continue with Spieren voor Spieren. In two years, the European Football Championship would be held in Holland and Belgium – a great opportunity for another great fundraising event. We approached Louis van Gaal, the then head coach of the Dutch football team, and his wife to become ambassadors for Spieren voor Spieren.

Louis and Truus' Column

Why we actively support Spieren voor Spieren

Louis[5] and Truus van Gaal
Ambassadors for Spieren voor Spieren

It was in 1994, Ajax was reaching the world top and all of a sudden, we were approached by Michael Goeman. Michael's generation of football players includes Bryan Roy, Richard Witschge and the de Boer brothers – the potato-chip generation – as Michael, in his humorous way, described them. Michael was no libero or striker. Michael wrote a letter to Ajax because he wanted to join the club of his dreams, having finished his HAVO exams. He asked, "Could I do some practical work?" We were still situated in the old "de Meern" stadium. There he was in his wheelchair; he had Werdnig-Hoffman, a severe form of muscular dystrophy. He had never been able to kick a ball himself. I saw a boy who wanted to do everything to make his dream come true, and that is why I did everything to help him. This boy had to join Ajax. He started behind the telephone, and later got a permanent job. He performed very well, and I was so happy and proud for him.

In 2000, Truus and I were approached to become ambassadors of the Spieren voor Spieren Foundation. We did not have to think very long. With Michael in the back of our minds, it was not very difficult to decide. It is fantastic to see that children with muscular dystrophy often have a top sport mentality. It is also great to see that people with healthy muscles are prepared to give themselves for children who are less fortunate. It does not matter, whether it is during a gala fundraising dinner, or during my fixed conversations with radio 538 DJ Edwin Evers, or during a lecture or other event, every time it strikes me how involved and engaged these people are in helping the less privileged. The wonderful interaction between the top sports figures and the people with a muscular dystrophy is just fantastic. That is why we are so proud to be ambassadors, and we will continue to be for a long time.

Before becoming Head Coach of Bayern Munich Louis van Gaal was Technical Director and Head Coach of Ajax, the Dutch National Team and FC Barcelona. He has won all the prizes that can be won at the club team level. Becoming world champion with a national team is still on his wish list.

During the post-mortem of the first event, we listed the lessons learnt and reached a clear conclusion that the next time we could not start with a shortage of cash in our accounts. We needed to ensure that we had sufficient cash at the start to fulfil our financial obligations. A few changes were made to the Spieren voor Spieren Board, but I was asked to stay on as Chairman and remained for another six years.

By the beginning of 2000, I held the number two position in Foods and Beverage Europe (see Appendix II). In order to properly organize the next big event for Spieren voor Spieren, I figured that I would need about three weeks. But where do you find three free weeks? I always use my full vacation entitlement to spend with Renée and the children. And, we had already made our arrangements for 2000.

I decided to ask my boss, Roy Brown, the Business Group President, for three weeks of unpaid leave. I crossed the corridor, walked into his office, closed the door and sat down at his desk. There was nothing unusual about this. We did this every day when we were both in the office. I explained to him where we were with the preparations of the new Spieren voor Spieren fundraising event, but that an enormous amount of work still needed to be done. Spieren voor Spieren only had one full-time (paid) employee. I needed to be involved in important parts of the TV script, the fundraising and the management of the relationships with KNVB and its sponsors. Finally, I asked him for three weeks of unpaid leave.

For a moment, he was silent. It felt like hours to me. Then he said, "No, we are not going to do that." I thought my heart was going to stop. I had a terrible sinking feeling, and all kinds of thoughts were racing through my mind, "What a jerk … typical … just thinking about the business, not caring for his people. What do I do now? Resign?"

Then he said, "Kees, you take as much time as you need to ensure the event is highly successful. Take the time when you need it and you will be fully paid. Forget this nonsense about unpaid leave. I know you are fully committed. I know you will take the necessary actions to ensure your business stays on track. You will delegate a few more things. That is good. You need to learn to do that. So that is one benefit. The second benefit is that you will develop a completely new network and you will see and learn things you will not see and learn at Unilever. This is good for you, good for your development and good for Unilever."

I almost flew over his desk to kiss him. What a great guy. He really cares. How wrong I was with my split-second thoughts about him.

When put in a similar situation, I remembered Roy Brown

In 2007, my personal assistant, a bright young financial manager, approached me about Unilever's partnership with the World Food Programme. He was so impressed with the initiative that he wanted to spend six weeks working for the organization in Indonesia to help them with logistics and distribution. He had spoken to people at the WFP, and he knew they could use him. While I did wonder how I would cope without him, it only took me a few seconds to tell him that it was a great idea, that he would learn so much and that he should go for this once-in-a-lifetime opportunity. And so he went, had a great time and afterwards he became an even more convincing ambassador for Unilever.

REFLECTIONS

For the *Power of Balance* project, Tom Malnight and I interviewed, as mentioned, some 80 CEOs from around the world. One of the key insights was that leaders need to have the ability to face the consequences of their situation and the courage to make difficult decisions. Most of today's senior executives, CEOs and board chairs are very much occupied by their jobs. The pressures are horrific. The challenges they and their organizations are facing are huge. It is not surprising that the lion's share of their time is being absorbed by work, work and even more work. It seems that the busier they get the more they can cope with. They want to come across as determined individuals who know where they want to take their organizations. There is no space for allowing people to understand them or their personal motives or drivers. There is no way they will admit to a mistake, and they find it difficult to talk about their family or their personal circumstances. They might come across as too soft – it would be a sign of weakness.

Through my experience with my son Bart, I have discovered that this type of behaviour by leaders is utter nonsense. When you have your priorities right, people perceive you as a more human leader. By tearing down the wall between your work and your private life, making it clear that there are family moments and business moments, you gain respect. You will be perceived as more mature, grounded and authentic. Together, these elements will make you a more effective leader, and people will be more prepared to follow you and accept the direction you are taking them in, however inconvenient this might be at times.

When I teach this subject in the IMD classroom, I am often asked if a person needs to experience a personal "drama" before he or she comes to the realization that things are dramatically out of balance and that some far-reaching steps need to be taken to bring life back under control. Strangely enough, I find myself answering with a firm but softly spoken, "Yes." I am afraid that we do indeed often need a wake-up call to really understand that we have to face reality and, more importantly, do something about it. However, it is my hope that by sharing my experiences, I will encourage my audience to ask themselves the following:

- Am I really in control of my own destiny?
- Do I need to rebalance part of my life, or maybe even my entire life?
- Am I achieving what I set out to achieve; will I leave something meaningful behind, something I can be really proud of?

In the following chapters, I will provide some ideas on how one can create the circumstances to be able to answer these questions.

Notes

[1] By Bain News Service (Public Domain), via Wikimedia Commons.

[2] Bundesarchiv, Bild 183-48082-0005 / CC-BY-SA.

[3] Adapted from Kolata, Gina. "Reanimated 'Junk' DNA is Found to Cause Disease." *International Herald Tribune*, August 21-22, 2010.

[4] Heartbrand is the heart-shaped logo that appears on all of Unilever's ice creams internationally.

[5] Photograph of Louis van Gaal by: Fred Joch, Poing, Germany.

Acting responsibly:
Bringing values to life

2

Up to this point, I have focused on how my professional and personal lives overlap and how that has driven me to act in more socially responsible ways. In this chapter, I will describe the merger between my values and Unilever's values. The stories I will share illustrate what "creating real purpose", "living your values" and "commitment" mean for me.

The stories will also provide a few insights into the relationship between business and society, with particular emphasis on the importance of engaging the people within your organization to care for society and the environment in which they operate. As long as there are hundreds of millions of people dying from starvation, obesity, pandemics, warfare and natural disasters, companies need to take responsibility for making the world a better place.

ALMERIA: HOW THE REST WAS WON

In April 2001, I took over Unilever's Ice Cream and Frozen Foods Europe (ICFE)

> **insight**
>
> *As long as there hundreds of millions of people dying from starvation, obesity, pandemics, warfare and natural disasters, companies need to take responsibility for making the world a better place.*

> **insight**
>
> *Bring your vision, mission statements and core values to life. Often these well-meaning statements become hollow phrases that are nicely framed and put on the walls of meeting rooms. This can be avoided by designing a process of co-creation that involves many people in the development of your mission and vision.*

business group. A short time later, we had our first leadership meeting in Ecoublay (see Chapter 3), where we agreed on the "must-win battles"[1] for the group, following which good progress was made on several fronts. The Heartbrand[2] was ready to be launched, strong ideas were developed for using the Knorr brand in frozen foods, and the Magnum brand went from strength to strength thanks to a combination of good advertising and the subsequent launch of a fantastic new innovation – the Magnum 7 Deadly Sins – which was both controversial and highly successful.

However, the implementation of some of the must-win battles was moving slowly – too slow for my liking – and I concluded that we had a problem with culture in the organization. There was no sense of urgency. There was too much in the way of debates, politics and personal agendas and not enough action.

Defining our values

A small team had been working hard to establish a number of unique values for ICFE, which had been discussed at length by the senior leadership team. The communications team had done a great job of visualizing the values through the introduction of a character called "Lady Ice". She would become the personification of ICFE's values.

Additionally, the top 100 members of the leadership team were engaged in agreeing on what would be acceptable and

> **... in this chapter**
> - Almeria
> - Hearts for Kids
> - Seefeld
> - Reflections

unacceptable behaviours in the new ICFE organization. There was broad consensus that we could only be successful in establishing the desired culture for the organization by being explicit about the desired behaviours. In the end, it would be the way we behaved and the way we lived – our values – that would determine the depths we could reach in building a great culture within the business group. The values that we agreed upon and which I have largely adopted as my own values and belief system were:

Sharing/caring/daring [3]

- Love and respect each other, our brands, our customers and our suppliers.
- Dare to take risks, be courageous, think outside of the box.
- Share information, successes and failures; create a feeling of togetherness in a great team.

Tight/loose

- For us, this was a friendlier way of saying "freedom within in framework". There were certain rules set by the

Lady Ice: Be the change you want to see

corporate centre that had to be followed (without discussion). Within those rules, the individuals were free to implement things their way.
- As we were moving the European business from a loose federation of fairly independent companies to an integrated European business (not company), it was important to make it crystal clear what would be done the European way and what would be left to the local operating companies. Of course, this initially created a series of negative reactions from "the old Barons" – the Chairmen of the large countries (Italy, UK and Germany).

Lean and mean

- We would have a lean, non-bureaucratic organization that could make decisions quickly. This would result in a pleasurable, stimulating workplace.
- "Mean" was our attitude towards costs. We did not like unnecessary spending. Initially, Unilever challenged our use of the word "mean" because it was counter to everything the company stood for. Unilever was a great company with its heart in the right place. Ultimately, however, it came to understand that we were using it in the context of unnecessary costs.

Simple/fast/pragmatic

- This was a clear expression about "how" we wanted to operate.
- It meant doing away with unnecessary complexity, the endless non-value-adding discussions and the sometimes academic, theoretical approaches towards strategy development and implementation. We had to become superb in what a colleague termed, "the art of implementation".

Trust and teamwork

- By respecting and listening to each other and working together, we could become so much stronger. This meant we had to learn from each other and invest in getting to know one another. When team members know they can trust each other, they become an unbeatable team.

ICFE had defined its way forward – its must-win battles, its values, its required behaviours. Now the challenge was to embed all of this in the organization. Even though I had great respect for my leadership team, I could not leave the implementation in their hands. We had to reach everybody – the different countries, the factories, the sales staff in remote villages – in a simple and convincing way. And, we had to do it fast. If I were to leave it to the functional heads and the country leaders, there was a risk that different interpretations would be communicated in different places at different times. So, I took on the task of finding a creative solution to reach all the people in the organization.

The big event

I wanted to engage the entire ICFE management team, some 1,500 people, in a memorable event to bring the values alive. The event would also provide the opportunity to launch the Heartbrand, welcome the Knorr brand into the frozen foods portfolio, kick-off of a corporate social responsibility (CSR) initiative and of course, inform the group about the behaviours that would be required to live our values.

I put together a team that consisted of Marianne Cool from our communications group, my secretary Lisette Lai-A-Fat, Professor Tom Malnight from IMD and me. We met with Signum Niehe, an agency we had previously worked with to organize corporate events, at the Sheraton in Schiphol. I had no clue what the budget should be, so I said that it would depend on the quality of their idea. Signum was not fazed by the large number of people involved – they had done bigger events. After a few exploratory questions, they left the meeting with a promise to come back with a response in a few weeks.

We were not impressed with the first few "safe" options they presented a few weeks later. But, then they brought us the exciting and revolutionary idea that we decided to go with. They proposed that we fly everyone to Almeria, a holiday

Different executions of ICFE's Heartbrand logo

beach resort in the south of Spain. It was off-season, so hotel rooms would not be a problem. Almeria had an airport where large charter planes could land. And, it was close to the Wild West movie sets that had been used to film some famous spaghetti westerns, such as *Once Upon a Time in the West, A Fistful of Dollars* and *The Good, the Bad and the Ugly*.

The sets had since been turned into a theme park for tourists, that was available for exclusive use. Signum Niehe proposed splitting the group into 50 teams and asking each team to write a script and shoot a two- to three-minute video clip expressing one of the behaviours. We would use 25 different sets, and each group would have a budget that they could use for props, costumes, make-up artists, stunt training, etc. Each team had to adhere to the following timetable:

- One hour to get to know each other (because we would group the people in multifunctional, multinational teams).
- One hour to write the script.
- A short time to divvy up the roles (actors, set builders, stuntmen, etc.).
- One hour to rehearse on the set.
- One hour to shoot the clip.
- One hour to clean up.

Signum would fly in 25 complete film crews with equipment from Holland and costumes and stunt actors from Madrid.

Manon, from Signum, convinced us that she could write an overall script that would connect the 50 clips. Overnight, the professionals would put all the clips together and add music and the connecting text. The next morning, the participants would watch the film about ICFE's values. We loved the idea, despite being deeply concerned about the logistics and the practicalities. But, now, at least, we had agreed to one part of the event. The next items on the agenda were the Heartbrand launch, integrating the Knorr brand into Unilever's frozen food portfolio and the CSR initiative, for which Signum had also developed some good ideas.

Upon arrival, everyone would be transported to the bullring in Almeria for the welcome act, which would consist of a horse show, flamenco dancing and speeches from the Brand Director Suzanna Luick and me. After a buffet dinner in the ring, a laser and music show would introduce the Heartbrand logo. In order to bring the new logo to life, the tempo of the show was designed to get our hearts beating. The following morning, everybody would be moved to the Wild West movie sets – by bus! I envisioned chaos, with 40 buses all leaving at the same time to go to a small village. Not to worry. The Mayor and the police had given us their full support. As soon as the recording was finished, the Knorr show would start. With Knorr, the proof of the pudding is in the eating, so the plan was to have a large banquet prepared by all the chefs who worked for Knorr in Europe. At the end of the evening, there would be an acrobatic show, in the spirit of *Cirque du Soleil*. After a short night's sleep, everyone would go to a large exhibition centre where the film would be shown to 1,500 people. Then, the concept of ICFE's CSR programme would be introduced in breakfast-show style with a presenter and some entertainment.

As you can imagine, we were deeply impressed with the programme – it was going to achieve exactly what we had aimed for. Though it was going to be pricey, I decided that it was worth it and gave the green light. The next big question was how we would make all of this happen. Unilever travel took care of the flight arrangements. Signum did the rest with the help of Marianne, Lisette and Bianca (Marianne's co-worker) from ICFE. Tom Malnight ensured that the content quality was great.

A major decision was to keep everything totally secret. Nobody, except the organizers, was supposed to know anything about the agenda. I sent out a personal invitation making it clear that this was going to be a must-attend (no apologies), high-impact event somewhere in Europe. People only had to be on time at an airport near them and bring light, warm clothes and wear tennis shoes; everything else would be included. Amazingly, we managed to keep it a secret to the day. Everybody knew that I was a keen sailor, so the tennis shoe instructions made them think that we would be sailing on big ships somewhere in the south.

Health, safety and security
Moving 1,500 people, including the Unilever Chairman, the Foods Director and several senior managers, to and from multiple locations (which included 40 buses twice a day and some 10 different hotels) in a country that was still encountering terrorist attacks were reasons enough to pay particular attention to health, safety and security. Fortunately, I had demanded a complete set of "what ifs" because with the exception of a plane crash and a terrorist attack, everything else that could happen, did happen:

- There were rainstorms and cold temperatures in a place where this kind of weather happens only 20 days per year.
- Due to heavy rain and exceptional winds, there were major delays and cancellations of flights in the Barcelona hub.
- Prince Claus of the Netherlands passed away.
- There was a series of small accidents during the recordings that required all three emergency ambulances to be used to transport participants to the hospital. Fortunately, only minor injuries were suffered.
- The Chairman of Unilever arrived late to deliver his speech.

Improvisation and brilliant anticipation

Due to the heavy winds, supper in the bullring would mean eating sand. So, early in the afternoon, the decision was made to move the dinner next door to a sports hall. While the authorities gave us permission to hold the dinner there, it was on the condition that we install a floor to protect the surface of the sports hall. We did not have enough people to lay the floor, move everything from the arena and create the right atmosphere, so the Mayor came up with a creative solution – he temporarily released 20 prisoners from the local jail to put the floor down. This created a rather strange atmosphere. There were heavily armed Guardia Civil in every corner and at every entrance to the hall, ensuring the prisoners, in jeans and blue shirts with their numbers on the back, did what they were supposed to do.

By the second part of the evening, the wind had died down, so the laser show and disco party took place in the bullring. However, the winds picked up again by the second evening, so the acrobatic act had to be cancelled. Since the agenda had been kept secret, nobody noticed that we had dropped it.

Recording the clips

On the day of the filming, I was driven to the Wild West village very early in the morning. Everything was in great shape and the temperatures were cool, which was lucky as I was wearing my *Lone Ranger*

Recording the Indian Chiefs clip with the ICFE leadership team

outfit. In the opening act of the event, I had to rescue Lady Ice (the personification of ICFE's values) from the hands of a group of bandits. I was on the roof of the bank in front of the village square, where all 1,500 managers were recovering from the shock of being in the Wild West. After rescuing Lady Ice, which included a lot of action – shooting, explosions, shouting – I addressed the team and gave the brief for the rest of the day.

It was great to see how much passion the teams put into the day; they fully absorbed themselves in expressing the acceptable and unacceptable behaviours in the most powerful and creative way.

They had no clue that a feature film would be produced overnight with the video clips; they had been led to believe that it was just a clip they could take home after the event.

I was asked to participate in two different video clips, including one where I was to play a homosexual who was in a relationship with a colleague. The other was with the leadership team, in which we formed a group of Indian Chiefs that banded together to declare war on the competition. We performed a real fire dance that became the opening scene of the movie. The fire dance also gave the implicit message that there were too many

Can-can dancers

chiefs and not enough Indians, which the audience picked up on.

Inspired by the environment, everyone's inner child was awakened. They all loved the dynamite explosions, gunfire and fist fighting. In the heat of the moment, one manager hit his colleague so hard that even a good beefsteak could not stop a beautiful black eye. In another instance, one of the female employees fell over on her high heels while she was playing the role of a

can-can dancer. She had quite a cut on her head, so was rushed to the hospital where she was immediately operated on by a famous surgeon who specialized in aesthetics. The surgeon was told by his staff that the employee was a famous actress, so he rushed in from a fishing trip on his free afternoon.

That evening, while the film directors were working through the night to get the movie ready for its premiere the following morning, we symbolically welcomed the Knorr brand into our frozen food portfolio with a mega cooking session using all of the Knorr products.

By the end of the evening, large posters had been put up in all the hotels announcing the world premiere the following morning of the film entitled *How the Rest was Won*, featuring a cast of 1,500 ICFE managers.

The last day: Caring for the children
Early in the morning on the third day of the Almeria event, the TV crew had completed the compilation of all the clips into a movie and the large theatre that had been created was quickly filling up. From the opening scene, the audience was entranced. They enjoyed watching their colleagues and had great fun and a good laugh as they observed 50 expressions of acceptable and unacceptable behaviour.

Of course, there was a power cut in the middle of the movie. Now what? We quickly decided to invite everyone who

was celebrating a birthday to come up on stage so their colleagues could wish them a happy birthday. The good thing about large gatherings is that there are always some people celebrating their birthday on any given day. That day five colleagues were celebrating their birthdays. After 10 minutes, the power came back on, and the film ran without further interruptions. At the end, we announced the fact that we had broken a world record – 24 hours from briefing to the world premiere of a two-hour feature film.

Poster for the movie: How the Rest was Won

The climax of the day was the breakfast show with the famous Dutch TV presenter, Vivian Boelen. One by one, different members of my team came on stage to be interviewed about the status of our must-win battles. A few leaders, including the Chairman of Unilever, were also interviewed. All made important statements in support of the new direction of the ICFE group.

At the end, it was my turn. I was convinced by the production company and my communications team that I had to look good in front of the camera, so I had to get up at 3:30 in the morning to get a full treatment from the chief make-up artist. She knocked on my door spot on time. I sat in front of the mirror, while she applied her powders and creams. She started by breaking a glass ampoule and spreading the contents on my face. My skin immediately shrank and I appeared five years younger. By the end, I had a lot of colour on my face and, for the first time in my life, mascara on my eyes. I had serious doubts about the consequences. All day, I felt as if my skin was going to crack at any moment. But, at least I now had an understanding of how artificial beauty can be.

As I came on stage, my nerves were on edge. I had rehearsed the presenter's questions in order to respond well, and then I had to deliver one of my best-ever closing speeches. The presenter asked a few simple questions that put me at ease. Via my involvement in the FSHD Foundation, she asked what I wanted to do to bring the ice cream heartbrand logo to life. I explained to the audience that we now had a heart on all our packaging and that millions of consumers would now see the heart and probably wonder why we had chosen it. I explained that a heart communicates that you care. You care for your consumers by providing them with great tasting, good quality products. But you should also care for the environment and the community. And wouldn't it be fantastic if we could make that heart beat for all of our stakeholders and our employees?

I then told the audience that I wanted all the people in our organization to start to care for the next generation. I wanted to launch a drive called "Caring for the Future of Our Children". My message to the managers was that every employee from the ICFE business would be given one day every year to dedicate to helping children in the neighbourhoods where our sites or offices were located. I gave a few examples, and then the presenter asked me an unrehearsed question, "Kees, how many people work in your organization?"

"15,000", was my reply.

"15,000! Do you know what that means? You have just donated 15,000 days of volunteer work to society. That is amazing, grandiose!"

It was only then that I realized just how big this initiative was. The presenter's emotional reaction brought the announcement to life. Then it was time to deliver my closing speech. I was very passionate and also emotional. The messages came across as being genuine. As a result, the audience gave a long standing ovation. Quite a few of my managers had tears running down their cheeks. The ICFE group of managers had become a large family – a real team that understood the sense of urgency and the need for change. Not only did they get the message, but they also got a real understanding for what needed to be done and, more importantly, HOW we were going to do it.

After the meeting, the communications team sent out a mailing to all employees, communicating the launch of "Caring for the Future of Our Children". The leaders received a full briefing deck that enabled them to get started. Of course, we involved the works councils and got the employees to select the projects that were close to the sites.

The early morning interview

HEARTS FOR KIDS

Immediately after returning to the Netherlands, we briefed our team in ICFE's head office following the storylines that were agreed to in Almeria. All the conclusions and key messages were cascaded throughout the organization. Of course, this also included the CSR initiative – Caring for the Future of Our Children. The reception was very positive. Several people volunteered to organize a project for the Netherlands. The first thing they agreed to do was make a list of possible projects.

Rotterdam Asylum Seekers Centre

After a few weeks, the group came back with a number of alternatives. There was one idea that everybody liked – supporting the Asylum Seekers Centre in Rotterdam. The Netherlands is a popular and attractive country for asylum seekers. Upon entry, they go to a "camp" where they have to stay until their case has been heard by a judge, who will either accept their request and grant a work permit or reject it and the people concerned will be transported back to their home country. This procedure can take a very long time. Children are often involved, and they have to stay in the camp with their families. There is nothing for them to do in the camp, so they become isolated from what is going on in the real world.

Our team agreed with the local authorities that we would refurbish a classroom in the camp. We would

insight

If you really want to reap the benefits of your CSR initiatives, ensure that, in principle, all of your employees participate in the project – not by donating money, but through active engagement.

completely redo it, paint it, furnish it with tables, stools, computers and games, and provide it with access to the internet. It became quite a project, and it required a number of people from our office who had to help with the painting, cleaning, fundraising and teaching. I was impressed by the number of people who were prepared to participate as volunteers for the project. Of course, I put my name on the list to participate as a painter.

As the project was taking shape, I had the unexpected pleasure of being taught how to paint a door by a charming junior secretary. I have to admit that I love do-it-yourself projects, and I have some experience with painting and laying carpets. But during the briefing session, I pretended to be an amateur. It was great to hear her professional, clear instructions. In a very charming way, she explained to me – her ultimate boss – how to paint one of the doors. Every now and again, she came to check my work. All of a sudden, our established roles and relations had taken on a new order, and it brought home the message that people can do so much more than the jobs they have been hired

to do. It opened my eyes, and I promised myself that I would be more daring in giving people increased responsibilities sooner by placing them in different roles and testing them out. It is our responsibility as leaders to bring people's talents to the forefront through developmental opportunities so that they can excel.

We also organized a weeklong summer camp for the children. Because the number of children was rather small, we extended it with an additional 10 underprivileged youngsters from Rotterdam. During the week, a small drama involving one of the little girls unfolded. She was crying uncontrollably. We finally discovered that

insight

Be more daring in giving people more responsibility sooner – it is our responsibility as leaders to bring these talents to the forefront through developmental opportunities in which they can excel.

she had lost her earring, and if she went home without it, she would be physically punished. She was so afraid of the punishment that she was shaking all over. The solution was simple. We took her to a shop, found something that she considered identical and bought it for her – a small gesture that would avoid a traumatic experience for a little girl.

Thanks to the project, I noticed that people in the office were starting to interact with each other in a different way. There were two reasons to which I attributed this change in behaviour – the common purpose of helping children in need was very rewarding and the employees got to know each other in completely different circumstances. It built the team chemistry.

The 2003 management conference
At the beginning of each year, Unilever organized a senior leadership conference in a special location (which depended on the quality of the results) to present each business group's results and Unilever's overall results. In February 2003, the venue was the Van Nelle Factory, a historic building in the centre of Rotterdam that used to be a tobacco and tea factory.

Promoting the new Heartbrand

insight

Build team chemistry by involving your employees in corporate social responsibility projects. A common purpose of helping someone or something in need is very rewarding and employees get to know each other in completely different circumstances.

Next to presenting the 2002 results, the main purpose was to announce the official launch of the Heartbrand to the shareholders, the press, the trade and consumers. A huge press conference was planned with live links to the different newswires. I also had to do a few live interviews, the most difficult being with the Spanish business network, in Spanish!

The other topic on the agenda was the different activities in the different countries under the banner of, "Caring for the Future of Our Children". For two hours, we listened to selected stories of the many initiatives that the ICFE organizations had undertaken. One that I will always remember was the story about a little girl who was kidnapped on her way home from the railway station. It happened somewhere in Kingston upon Thames (UK), possibly in front of our offices. The poor little girl was abused and then killed. The police entered our offices in big numbers to interview everyone in the event that someone had noticed something strange outside. This immediately led to the start of a campaign to help children deal with the

dangers on the street. Together with the police, the local authorities and specialists, our team developed a programme for schools. Our employees took turns teaching these programmes, and they organized fundraising events to finance the programme.

Another story with great impact came from our Turkish colleagues about the way they engaged in the aftermath of the large earthquake in Turkey. They basically helped with finding caring homes for the new young orphans.

At the end of the conference, I handed out some prizes – a financial contribution – to the best initiatives.

Hearts for Kids Foundation
One day after launching the Heartbrand, I got a visit from six young Unilever managers. They were all participants in Carrousel, Unilever's initial training course for young graduates. They wanted to participate in the Heineken Regatta, a sailing event in St. Maarten in the Caribbean. Their idea was that they would wear a T-shirt with the heart logo and that I would pay for their flights and boat rental. My first reaction was to laugh in their faces. I told them they had no idea what I was trying to do with the Heartbrand and that their outrageous idea would not be supported. Disappointed faces were staring at me! So, I told them that I might consider helping them if they did something special for the children of St. Maarten. I have a

Hearts for Kids logo

cousin who is a doctor in St. Maarten, and he had made me aware of some of the issues on the island. After I explained my intentions with the Heartbrand and gave them a little lesson on core values, the group left my office.

A week later, I found a really good proposal on my desk. The group would organize some fundraising events and all the funds they generated would be directed towards some much-needed medical equipment for the paediatrics department at a hospital in St. Maarten. The deal we agreed to was that I would pay their airfare if they met the target I set for them. They did, and off they went. In the meantime, they had created the "Hearts for Kids" Foundation.

I liked this name much better than "Caring for the Future of Our Children". With a very low budget, they had also created a fantastic logo for the newly created foundation. The boat they had rented for the regatta was renamed "Hearts for Kids". They performed

miserably in the regatta, but to everybody's surprise, they were called on stage directly after the overall winner was honoured. They had won a special press prize for the impressive way they had created awareness of the problems on St. Maarten. It was not all about luxurious yachts that participated in glamorous sailing events, with good food, good drinks and post-event parties. The island had many poor people with children who were receiving a poor education and below-standard medical care. I don't have to explain how proud the group was and what this experience meant for their professional development.

A year later, they wanted to participate in the regatta again. I agreed, but this time, the deal was that the target would be raised by tens of thousands of euros. They agreed, and this time they planned to raise funds for a school in support of both educational materials and sports facilities. Not only did they get recognition for their community work, they also sailed better and came second in their class.

Kilimanjaro and Tanzania

The group that participated in the Heineken Regatta was also given the objective of making their initiative sustainable. I felt this kind of initiative was a brilliant way to

Hearts for Kids team, Heineken Regatta, St. Maarten

Maarten's Column

Inner growth

Maarten Smits
Trainer, Coach & Therapist
Inmensgroeien – www.inmensgroeien.nl

In 2002, I was a management trainee with Unilever. There was a group of us who shared a passion for Unilever and for sailing. In the pub, we hatched the idea of sailing in the Heineken Regatta together, and getting Unilever to pay for it somehow or other. We chose Kees as our self-appointed sponsor: his job was at a level where he could take this kind of decision and finance it; besides that, he was an avid sailor himself. We took our chances and sent him an e-mail saying that we had a business proposition for him and that we needed just 30 minutes to explain it. We thought we would promote Ola with its new logo in exchange for our expenses.

We were amazed when we were invited to Kees's office in Rotterdam just two weeks later. And we were even more surprised to hear his reply when we got to the final slide of our presentation asking "are you on board?". Okay, he said, but: we're not going to do this your way. Kees wanted "his" 16,000 employees to broaden their horizons and to contribute to society. He made the following proposal: we had to at least double his investment in us and give the money to a local cause. He asked us for a concrete proposal within two weeks. The result was the Hearts for Kids Foundation, for which we collected 50,000 euros for the local hospital in the first year.

Our own hedonistic motivation got turned into a situation that was very nourishing for all parties. The hospital got two heart monitors for the paediatrics department; Kees created a permanent platform for new trainees that is still making meaningful contributions to society at a European level, and I was personally moved by the difference you can make by looking beyond your own self-interests. It's a lesson I will never forget, and I am still hugely proud of the "Spirit & Style Award" we received from the Heineken Regatta organisation for our work. To use your passion to make a contribution to your work and to society has enriched me as a human being enormously.

Right now, I work as a trainer, coach and therapist at InmensGroeien, which takes inner growth as the starting point for personal and corporate transformations.

inmens groeien

educate the new generation of Unilever managers about values and the importance of caring for the communities in which Unilever operates. They established a way to engage the Carrousel participants and to find a few aficionados to take the reins of the Foundation and propose new ways of bringing "Hearts for Kids" to life.

The second generation climbed Mount Kilimanjaro after building an orphanage at the bottom of the mountain. The third generation got more than 100 people to participate in the Amstel Gold Race, a cycle event in the south of the Netherlands. They even got me to ride 125 km in the race.

I never realized how many places one's body could hurt after just five hours of cycling. They were successful in raising the respectable sum of €160,000 for water tanks for six schools in Tanzania. The initiative lives on, and the fifth generation of young managers has submitted a proposal to my successor Doug Baillie, who has taken it to the next level, rolling it out to other European countries and supporting the World Food Programme.

The World Food Programme

Every year more than six million children die from hunger – that is, 17,000 children a day.[4] This is an unacceptable number, and food companies like Unilever must become part of the solution.

When I was Foods Director of Unilever, we signed a cooperation contract with UNICEF. Except for the Indian project –

Amstel Gold Race

Partnership for Child Nutrition (PCN) – not a lot materialized. Through our internal corporate affairs department, we entered into a contract with the World Food Programme (WFP). Alan Jope, the global category leader for Spreads liked the idea of doing something with our family brands in margarine – Rama and Blue Band – which are enriched with essential nutrients for children. The Spreads group reached an agreement with the WFP, consisting of a payment in kind and a series of cause-related marketing programmes [5]. Unilever would donate a few eurocents to the WFP for every pack of margarine it sold. This meant that the consumer would partner with Unilever in providing children

in underdeveloped countries with full school meals.

Because the agreement with the WFP was made at the Unilever corporate level, buy-in from the country organizations was low. Personally, I liked the idea. The possibilities were good for engaging our people in the programme. When I heard about the "Walk against Hunger", my attention was triggered. I asked the European communications department to find out if we could participate and if we could support the WFP through this organization. The team came back with the message that TNT, the Dutch post office, which had been the main sponsor of the first walk the previous year, would love us

to come on board and help make the event even bigger.

At one of the corporate centre's quarterly results briefings, I pitched the event and asked for volunteers to walk with me on Mother's Day, a perfect day to walk with your family and raise awareness of the millions of children dying from hunger. It was a 5 km walk through Rotterdam. Erica Terpstra, president of the Dutch Olympic Committee, welcomed the thousands of walkers and together with the CEO of TNT, Peter Bakker, and me, the three of us made a symbolic start to the walk by rolling a gigantic globe forward.

This was the first time in my life that I had participated in a demonstration, and it had quite an impact on me. Everybody was wearing the same T-shirt, and the people on the sidelines were interested in and sympathetic to our cause. It was great. And the television coverage helped spread the news beyond Rotterdam. The same walk took place in many European cities, but there were few Unilever participants outside of the Netherlands. In London, none of my colleagues on the Unilever Executive was able to participate. It was clear that we had to increase awareness for 2008 to get more of our leaders to lead by example.

We produced a very powerful video to build enthusiasm among our employees. It was so good that I got very emotional when I saw it for the first time. I suggested putting it on the air straight away as an advertisement in all the cinemas in the

Netherlands, informing the consumer about our WFP initiative. Sadly, the marketers told me that the quality of the video was not good enough and that it was not 100% aligned with the positioning statement of the margarine brand. I was not happy. I loved that commercial and felt that we had missed a great opportunity to show Unilever from a completely different perspective to a large audience. These marketers still had a lot to learn!

Sponsorship of the Austrian Alpine Ski Team

Apart from ice cream, the ICFE's frozen foods business in Western Europe was sizeable with over €2 billion in turnover in 2000. Well-known products included fish fingers, spinach, peas, pizzas and ready-to-eat meals and side dishes. They were sold under the Iglo brand in all countries except Italy, where the Findus brand was still used, and England and Ireland, where the Birds Eye brand was being used. The business was characterized by slow growth and lower-than-Unilever-average EBIT (earnings before interest and taxes) margins.

With no pan-European approach to marketing and innovation, every country did more or less its own thing. Italy and Austria were performing better than average. It was against this background that the Austrian Ice Cream and Frozen Foods Company entered into a sponsorship deal with the Austrian Ski Federation. A three-year contract was negotiated by the local

The Herminator's amazing comeback

The Unilever marketers in Austria were quite lucky. The years around the turn of the century were the best years ever for the Austrian downhill skiers. Between Stephan Eberharter and Hermann Maier, they won almost everything – the World Cups for downhill, giant slalom and the combination all went to Austria. On top of that, a few young skiers brought in good results in the slalom and other disciplines. The members of the ski team were Austria's national heroes. And they were all pretty down-to-earth, but passionate, athletes. There was no glamour, just the pure joy of winning.

At the height of his career, Maier had a near fatal motorcycle accident. The doctors wanted to amputate his leg. He refused. In order to save his leg, he had to drink lots and lots of water. His willpower was so strong that despite almost drowning himself in water, he was able to save his leg. And his recovery would go down as a miracle, when he shocked the skiing world 22 months later with an amazing World

Cup Super-G victory in the Hahnenkamm-Rennen in Kitzbühel in 2006. The Herminator was back!

The story still gives me the shivers. I find it amazing that someone can be so passionate about his sport that he gives up everything, goes through hell in terms of pain and suffering and fights his way back to the absolute top. He deserves deep respect. I wish it were possible to instil that kind of passion in all employees. What a difference it would make.

Watch it on YouTube
Maier's World Cup Super G Win in Kitzbuhel in 2006

insight
If only you could find a way to instil Maier's kind of passion in your employees. What a difference it would make to your organization.

Chairman Klaus Rabbel. The clothing of the men's downhill team would carry the Iglo logo, and the team would be available for advertising outings. On top of that, Iglo got the main sponsorship of a number of ski events in Austria. It was a good deal for a reasonable amount of money.

Making the sponsorship work
It is an unwritten rule in the world of marketing that a sponsor has to spend twice the sponsorship amount in marketing

activities to get the benefits from the sponsorship. Iglo's Austrian management came forward with an interesting approach. One of the key characteristics of "quick frozen foods" (QFF) is that all the vitamins and nutrients stay in the product; they do not get lost. This means that QFF products are actually fresher than the fresh produce that you buy in the market. In the past, the Unilever frozen foods companies had run famous campaigns showing how peas were harvested and then sent directly to the factory to be "quick frozen" in order to keep their nutrients. Austria developed the "Ess was gescheits" idea. Literally translated this means "Eat something good". In colloquial Austrian German, this has the double meaning of good taste, good reliable food and good for your body. The idea was that the company would shoot three commercials showing the ski team members leaving for their training camp. In the commercials, the mother of all-round skier Stephan Eberharter was kissing her son goodbye and, as all mothers do, she whispered some last-minute advice in his ear – "Be careful and ess was gescheits". She even went so far as to call her son on his mobile at inconvenient moments during the training. And, every time she said, "Ess was gescheits". It got to the point where Eberharter's team members were shouting, "Ess was gescheits" every time his phone rang.

Kitzbühel

As the new boss, I was invited to Kitzbühel to see our Iglo skiers in action during the Hahnenkamm-Rennen. Renée and I arrived at the hotel on Thursday evening.

insight

Sometimes the boss has to do weird things to gain the respect of his or her employees and to show commitment to a particular cause.

The entire ski team was staying at the same hotel. The first surprise came when we entered our room and found two complete Iglo ski outfits – hats, gloves, pants, anoraks, scarves and sunglasses. The outfits were bright green and ultra white with a little bit of red. They had huge Iglo logos and the "Ess was gescheits" slogans in big letters on every part of the outfit. Renée and I would become walking advertisements in the glamorous streets of Kitzbühel. The second surprise was that the famous former ski racer, Franz Klammer, would take me down the

horrific Streif the following day. I did it. But, I barely survived. I am a good skier, but this was almost beyond my abilities. It had rock solid, icy slopes and was steeper than anything I had ever seen before. I was so frightened and holding my poles so tightly that if it weren't for my gloves, my nails would have dug into my palms. My respect for the professionals increased significantly. The third surprise was the message that I was a member of the Iglo team that was going to participate in the charity run on the last part of the downhill track immediately after the finish of the

Kitzbühel Charity Run at the Hahnenkamm-Rennen

I was scared to death, but I did it

downhill race. The good news was that many other celebrities were participating, such as Olympic skiers, DJs and Formula 1 drivers. To get up the slope you had to take a slow old-fashioned anchor lift. In our bright green outfits, Klaus Rabbel and I went up the slope. Everybody recognized the brand – not us. Hundreds of people lined up along the sides of the lift started to chant our "Ess was gescheits" slogan.

This was going to be my first ever ski race since I was 12 years old in ski classes in Switzerland. Now I had to perform in front of 35,000 spectators and it would be shown live on television. I remember the speaker, announcing my appearance, commenting that I was most likely the first Dutchman to race down the Streif (only part of it, but it was steep enough). To my delight, I managed the gates pretty well and came flying through the finish to be interviewed immediately by the television station. Of course, I managed to get one ski with the brand name on it in front of the camera. Sometimes the boss has to do weird things to gain the respect of his people and to show his commitment to a particular cause.

The 100-hour programme

In 2003, Andre van Heemstra, the HR director on the Unilever Board, invited me to dinner. He said I would meet some interesting people and do him a favour by attending this dinner. At the time, I was President of ICFE. He gave me no clue why I was being invited or what impact these people could have on the bottom line of my business.

insight

Four concepts I learnt from the 100-hour programme included:
1) Liking yourself
2) Unconditionally loving everybody else
3) Providing space for employment
4) Giving recognition/positive encouragement.

When I arrived at the small table for four in Unilever's immense board dining room, I was introduced to the other two guests – a rabbi and a Goan opera singer. The conversation went in the direction of creating a better world. What better group to have this discussion – two Christians, a Jew and a Muslim. It soon became evident that we shared quite a few common values.

Coincidentally, I had attended a performance of the opera singer, Paul Vincent, the previous year. Paul explained his vision of creating world peace by taking all the children in the world through a short but well-defined training programme that would teach them basic values in a powerful way. I was sceptical, but he was convincing and passionate so I wanted to know more.

He had developed a 100-hour course that would be taught over a few months to school kids between 6 and 14 years. Paul was so convinced about the effectiveness of the programme that he planned to stop singing for a couple of years to devote his full time to it. Still noticing my scepticism, he offered to take me through 10 hours of the programme on condition that I would be open-minded and, more importantly, that I would participate in all exercises. It sounded like a good proposition to me.

When Paul came to my office for the first of 10 one-hour lessons, it was not difficult to be impressed. Every hour was clearly structured from start to finish. And, there was homework! The first lesson was about personal relationships. I had to draw a couple of concentric circles and put my real friends in the inner circle. In the next circle, I had to include people who were not as close and so on until I reached the outer circle where I had to put people that I really did not like. The outcome was a little bit of a shock, but the real shock came when I got my next round of homework. I had to choose someone from the outer ring, make contact and bring that person closer to my inner ring. In subsequent classes, Paul taught me the importance of liking all aspects of yourself – physical and emotional. For the physical part, I had to train by standing naked in front of the mirror every day, telling myself how great I looked. This took some courage, but eventually, I decided I looked great.

Four concepts I learnt during the programme included: 1) like yourself, 2) unconditionally love everybody else, 3) provide space for employment and 4) give recognition/positive encouragement. The more I thought about the concept of unconditional love, the more it grew on me. The concept is so rich and powerful. Paul and I had a long talk about a young guy who shot several of his schoolmates dead in the US. I found it unacceptable to show tolerance for his deed. Paul argued that I should ask myself why he did it. What happened to him in his youth? Was he put under too much pressure? Did he have friends? Could his deed have been avoided if he had been loved, respected and appreciated?

Paul had a strong point and it brought to mind two guest speakers at IMD who told the story of a young man who had been shot dead while delivering pizza. The killer's grandfather and the victim's father were telling the story. Both were from very different backgrounds. In the beginning, they did not have a relationship. Though the father of the victim mourned his son, he saw two victims. So he decided to forgive and reach out to the grandfather of the killer. Together they decided to learn from the tragedy. Now, they travel the world campaigning against useless violence. Forgiving is one thing, prevention another. After listening to this story, it reminded me of Paul Vincent and the concept that we need more unconditional love. Only then will we be able to stop all the unnecessary wars, riots and violence. Maybe Paul's vision is a better weapon in the war against terror than the current reality.

insight

When you reflect on it, there is incredible power in the concept of unconditional love.

SEEFELD: WINTER OLYMPICS

ICFE's business results in 2003 called for a real celebration, and the plan was to hold a celebratory event in Seefeld. Unilever's overall results, however, were no cause for celebration, so my superiors asked me to reconsider my plans for Seefeld. I did reconsider the plans, and very much to the dismay of Unilever's senior leadership, I stuck to the idea of Seefeld.

Young participant from Kosovo

Seefeld was chosen as the special location for the event, since I often fantasized about bringing the Winter Olympics to the Netherlands. But, probably the real reason is that it was my dream to organize an Olympic event, and Seefeld gave me my chance. The organizing committee had come up with the idea of an ICFE Winter Olympics. During the Kitzbühel Hahnenkamm-Rennen, I was deeply impressed by the quality of the food, the entourage and the entertainment. So, we asked the same people to organize our event. Our Austrian Chairman was instrumental in making it happen. We also managed to get the entire Austrian ski team and their coaches to come to the event – guys like Eberharter, Maier and Strobl, were all present.

We tied the event into the Hearts for Kids initiative by asking every company in each country in our business group to organize some fundraising activities to pay the minimum €5,000 entrance fee to participate in the Olympics. Simply transferring company money was not allowed; each country had to raise the money. The total amount raised would be donated to SOS Children's Villages during the last evening of the event.

We also invited about 20 children from an Austrian SOS Village to participate in the event. One of the children was still suffering from a bullet wound he had received during his escape from Kosovo. Each country had a team, strengthened by an Austrian skier and two SOS villagers. The instruction to the teams was to give these children the day of their lives. Each of the children got a shirt from the Austrian ski team with all their signatures. After a super day, which concluded with a ski show by the local ski school instructors, we handed over a cheque for €186,000 – much higher than expected – to the director of the SOS Children's Villages organization.

The event coincided with Niall FitzGerald's retirement as Co-Chairman and my promotion to the Board of Unilever. It was a perfect way for me to terminate my role as President of the ICFE group, knowing that the Hearts for Kids project was really alive and that SOS Children's Villages could build their village in Kosovo.

Children from the SOS Children's Villages

REFLECTIONS

The mission of every company should include a statement about the maximization of total value, not just shareholder value. This will ensure that a company does not become an isolated silo, only satisfying shareholder needs or, even worse, the expectations of the financial analysts. Instead, a company should be aware of its impact on society and take the necessary measures to care for the interests of all stakeholders. Only then, does a company earn the licence to operate. To do so, leaders in organizations must become more values-driven and demonstrate a real purpose and commitment to acting in socially responsible ways. In the wise words of one of my bosses, "If you are there, helping the people in need, they will remember you forever. They will remember the name of the company and the brand. And they will become your most loyal customers."

> **insight**
>
> *When you help people in need, they will remember you forever. They will remember the name of the company and the brand. And they will become your most loyal customers.*

Notes

[1] Killing, Peter, Thomas Malnight with Tracey Keys. *Must-Win Battles: How to win them, again and again.* Harlow, UK: Pearson International Learning, 2005.

[2] Heartbrand is the heart-shaped logo that appears on all of Unilever's ice creams internationally.

[3] Borrowed with pride from the old Best Foods organization, which used these values before being acquired by Unilever. It is interesting to note that when you read about values in the literature, you often come across the advice that organizations should "steal" with pride. In my opinion, "borrowing" has a nicer connotation. When you borrow an idea, you honour the other party by recognizing them and their good idea. Borrowing also implies that you will give something back in return.

[4] http://www.wfp.org/content/hunger-kills-17000-children-day (accessed 15 June 2010)

[5] Cause-related marketing is a type of marketing that involves cooperation between a for-profit business and a not-for-profit organization for mutual benefit.

Moving beyond the comfort zone: Leading with courage

3

In the previous chapters, I have focused on the relationships and the overlap between work, family, business and society. In this chapter, the focus will shift to the leader as an individual – how he or she leads, looks after himself or herself. We are all constantly facing new challenges and new situations where we need to act and make decisions. When change is required, we need to take the necessary steps to prepare the organization through a process of co-creation, involvement and engagement. Only then can we expect commitment and successful implementation.

Two of the examples in this chapter illustrate how I have struggled and dealt with change management situations. Another story describes how you can sometimes find yourself in a position where you have to take the lead and act alone rather than follow the ideal process. The final story in the chapter is about turning people's perceptions around and getting people on side. These last two examples really drove home my realization that it can sometimes be lonely at the top.

ECOUBLAY: DEFINING OUR MUST-WIN BATTLES [1]

Even before I took over our Ice Cream and Frozen Foods Europe business group in April 2001, I knew we had a problem. An employee survey showed that the people in the business felt it was lacking strategic focus

at the top. Apparently, leadership would be banging on the table one day saying, "We will launch a product everywhere, with the same brands, the same proposition", and the next day, one person would do one thing and another would do something else. There was no teamwork, no shared agenda and the country managers were each doing their own thing.

The second shock for me in that survey was the conclusion that the organization was not a place where it was safe to speak up. Speaking your mind about the real issues was not welcomed, and it was not an environment where risk-taking was encouraged. Making matters worse, there was little trust between the country operations and the corporate headquarters and, in fact, little trust between the countries themselves.

It was then that I decided we should be the first Unilever business to embark on a must-win battle (MWB) journey. Unilever's Executive had begun its own leadership journey earlier that year and management had decided the divisions should do the same thing. This was exactly what we needed. Even though our financial results were acceptable, I thought they would not stay that way for long. We had to change the status quo – the sooner the better.

The kick-off event: Engaging the team
I decided that we would invite about 45 people to the kick-off event. My objectives were to understand more about the business and the issues it faced, while at the same time establishing myself as the leader. I also hoped we would arrive at a

... in this chapter

- **Ecoublay**
- **Breaking paradigms**
- **The day of my board appointment**
- **Unilever Europe**
- **My sleepless night**
- **Reflections**

shared set of strategic priorities. So, up to a point, the more people who were there the better.

Before the event, I read a lot: the division's strategy, its operating framework, its magazines. I also chatted with a lot of people. I knew some of them already, but I did not know them in their current jobs. So I saw these talks as vital, as I needed to know what people were thinking about the business and each other. In my view, a leader has to listen to and be interested in

The arrival of the Olympic flag in Barcelona

In 1984, Barcelona won the bid to organize the 1992 Summer Olympics, beating other candidate cities, including Amsterdam. As a Dutchman, the son-in-law of the Vice President of the Dutch Olympic Committee, and as someone who had been approached by Max Gelders (the Chairman of McKinsey and the leader of the Dutch candidacy) to become a member of the Dutch organizing committee for the Olympics, I was of course pretty disappointed.

At the time, I could not know that I would be working in Barcelona from 1986 to 1990 as Marketing Director in the head office of Frigo, Unilever's ice cream and frozen products company. The four-year period we spent in Barcelona was, without a doubt, the most exciting and enjoyable time for our family. The combination of climate, culture, sports and people created the perfect circumstances for a dream assignment. We found a good English school for the boys, a lovely house in a small compound with neighbours like Gary Lineker – the famous English footballer – and a booming ice cream market.

The people of Barcelona embraced the Olympics. The city was transformed. The best minds were brought together to mastermind a great plan. Mayor Maragall, Catalonia's President Pujol, Ogilvy's Luis Bassat and the designer Javier Mariscal were some of the key players. It was clear that the Catalonians wanted to show the rest of Spain what they were capable of doing. All of a sudden, differences of opinion were buried. The political left and right started to cooperate, pragmatism was being applied everywhere. A telling example was when the number one and two candidate companies for organizing the opening ceremony decided to join forces a few hours before the final decision by the Spanish Olympic Committee. This move meant that the other competitors had no chance. And the result was truly memorable – the first really spectacular opening ceremony for the Olympics of the highest artistic calibre.

A few months after the Seoul Olympics ended in 1988, the Mayor of Seoul came to Barcelona to hand over the Olympic flag to the mayor of Barcelona. A huge event was staged in front of the Plaza de España. A million people were present. Top artists were performing. Everybody was enjoying this very special occasion. The weather was great. The grand finale was about to get started. The setting was ideal. The stage, which included a background set of steps up to a castle on a hill, was in front of the large fountains, where the water was "dancing" to the tune of the music. Totally unannounced, Montserrat Caballé (the opera diva) and Freddy Mercury (the lead singer of Queen) appeared on stage and began singing the "Barcelona" song. For fifteen minutes, their beautiful voices drifted over the audience – emotions were rising, the fountains were beautifully lit and as the song came to an end an enormous fireworks display emerged from behind the castle. It was an unbelievable setting. All of the elements – the dance, the music, the water, the fireworks – were in perfect harmony. The result — one million people were singing the Barcelona song with tears streaming down their faces. Everyone had goose bumps. It was a once-in-a-lifetime experience.

It proved to me that an event can have a powerful impact – alignment, emotional bonds – where differences become subordinate to the larger purpose. Sharing a common goal creates an incredible feeling of togetherness.

From then on, I used this insight at events like Ecoublay to motivate my own teams.

Watch it on YouTube
Freddy Mercury/Montserrat Caballé – Barcelona

the people in the organization. During the kick-off event, the plan was to share our "lifelines" and put all the taboo topics on the table for discussion. If we were going to succeed together, we had to develop trusting relationships.

My final step before the event was to work with the facilitators, walking through the programme that had been proposed by the corporate centre, and modifying it to suit my objectives. I had to make sure the programme focused on our needs, and was not just some standardized process mandated by head office.

The kick-off event was held in Ecoublay in an old chateau in the French countryside. There was no one else around, no fancy facilities, no formal meeting rooms, no PowerPoint presentations. The location was ideal for getting to know each other, putting difficult issues on the table, making choices and building the basis upon which we would work together for the next few years.

The night before the event began, we had dinner with Niall FitzGerald. Niall talked about what was happening in our overall business and the importance of the journey on which Unilever as a whole had embarked. He emphasized that this journey focused on both our businesses and our people. He called attention to a comment that one of the other executives had made: "Why are such talented people producing such mediocre results?" This was what we were there to address in the days and years ahead.

The facilitators: Mark Rutte, Tom Malnight, Annie McKee

Day1: Opening personal windows – the tent incident

On the first morning, we walked together through some woods to the ruins of a castle and that is where we started talking. It was my first real exposure to the group as a whole and I did not know what to expect. We began talking about our "hopes and fears" for the business. It was a strange environment for this discussion because you could feel what had once existed in those ruins and you could see what had become of it. Ice cream was a business in which Unilever had long been a market leader. Would we lead it to new levels of success or would we be responsible for its ruin? As we slowly pulled away from the

site in some old buses, the Chairman stood watching us. It was almost as if he were saying, "You're in charge now."

Our next stop was a small village. Here we sat and talked about our "myths and taboos" and how we, as a leadership team, operated and handled conflict. These discussions took place in small groups, and as each group turned in summaries of their discussions, I could see some real issues starting to come out.

> ## insight
> *Why is it that talented people sometimes produce mediocre results?*

A nice send off

Then we began to walk and suddenly we arrived at a large Turkish tent that had been prepared for us, which, of course, no one expected. This became the scene of a very important interaction. When the group kept telling me that "there wasn't a strategy" and that there was "no clarity about rules and responsibilities", I finally said, "But, I've read the strategy you wrote a few months ago; it was even signed by the European board members [2] individually." I added pretty strongly, "Do you always sign documents you don't agree with? If you do, then we will have a problem because this is something I find unacceptable."

Well, they found my comments unacceptable. As a result we had a fierce discussion with the group asking, "Who do you think you are saying those things to us?", and me replying, "If you are the kind of people who sign documents and then don't live up to your commitment, I will have great difficulty with that." After these emotional outbursts, we moved on to a cautious peace and decided to have lunch and come back to it later. During lunch, we had some light entertainment, but no one was paying attention. We were all thinking about the incident in the tent. After lunch, we agreed that we had to go back and reflect on what had happened and why.

I explained why it made me so angry to discover that people signed documents they couldn't remember and hadn't lived up to three months later. In my value system, a commitment is a commitment. If you do not want to commit, you do not; you speak up and remove yourself from the team of committed members. If necessary, HR will support you in your search for another position that you can commit to, either within Unilever or elsewhere. But if you do commit, I expect you to deliver against your commitment. My explanation helped the group understand why I was so disappointed with them. Did I have second thoughts about challenging the group so directly just a few hours into my tenure? No, it happened spontaneously. The only thing I regret is the strength of my reaction. Afterwards, everyone referred to the "tent incident" as the point that real change started to happen.

At the end of the day, we participated in an exercise called "personal lifeline", which led each of us to talk about who we are

Belly dancers: Light entertainment during lunch?

as individuals and some of the formative experiences in our lives. I went first. The others talked about their personal lifelines in small groups; I talked about mine in front of the entire group. It was a frightening prospect – talking about myself, my private life, my drivers – even though I was very proud of the shape my life had taken. I was nervous, but I liked the environment. It was informal and safe; people were lounging on sofas in a big circle and there were no outsiders. I felt comfortable even though there was some risk associated with exposing myself publicly. But, I firmly believe that as a leader, you have to be totally honest and authentic; people know when you are not being genuine. I always get emotional in these types of situations and people can sense that. By the end, I felt like I had run a marathon – I was physically and emotionally drained. That first day set the tone for the whole event.

Days 4–5: Committing to one agenda

Priorities only lead to action when they are understood, shared, owned, measured and monitored. So, during the last two days we

Peter's Column

Spreading the word

Peter Killing
IMD Professor
www.imd.org

In 2005, Tom Malnight, Tracey Keys and I wrote a book[3] based in part on Kees and Tom's must-win battle (MWB) experiences, which are presented in this chapter. Shortly thereafter, we wrote two lightly disguised cases[4] on the Ecoublay must-win battle offsite and the first time we taught these cases we videotaped Kees giving his personal views on the event.

The resulting cases and videotape have been well received at IMD and beyond. We have found that the MWB concept appeals to executives in large companies and small, profit and not-for-profit, and it crosses cultures easily. Most senior executives, regardless of the size of their organization, tell us that they have too many priorities and are looking for a way to create focus and energy. Thus, Kees's success with the must-win battle process is very appealing. They like the urgency that the phrase implies, and they can readily visualize the power coming from an offsite event when a team gets truly committed to no more than five shared key priorities.

Other executives, while appreciating the benefits of focus, state that the real attraction of the MWB process for them is the possibility of creating a better, more authentic team at the top, as Kees began to do with his personal lifeline story presented in reaction to the tent incident. These executives need to find a way to break through the personal barriers and organizational silos they are faced with every day, and see the MWB process as a potential solution.

Of course, the ultimate benefit of the MWB process is that you may be able to do both at the same time: create focus and build a stronger team at the top.

Our thanks go to Kees both for pioneering the MWB approach and for being so open in sharing his experiences so that others may learn.

chose the must-win battles for ice cream and developed a detailed understanding of what each MWB meant, the key issues we would have to address and the measures we would use to track progress. Most importantly, we chose the people who would be responsible for leading each battle. We purposely selected company Chairmen from different countries as the MWB leaders. Suddenly, managers who had only been looking out for the interests of their countries had a shared, collective task. In an instant, some thick silo walls began to break down. We needed a regional perspective to succeed in Europe, and these appointments were a major step in that direction. We created a team of interdependent leaders.

Towards the end of the session, we again discussed how we would work together, identifying the behaviours we would accept and not accept and what each of us would do to support our new agenda. The key questions were:

- What am I going to do differently from now on?
- What are the priorities that I am going to set for myself?
- What will I do more of and less of?

Every person in the room answered these questions out loud so that the others could hear what they had committed to.

For our final act at the offsite, I wanted to create a physical symbol of our new commitments. So we mounted a large piece of paper on a board in the middle of the room and said, "If you are committed, put your name and a message on the board. And if you are not committed, you can have a chat with the HR people who will find you another job within Unilever or elsewhere." This was a shock; it had never been done before. I was saying either you are with us as we try to change this business or find yourself another job. It made a huge impact.

I still remember the first person – James Hill – who stepped forward to put his message up. Then it was almost like an avalanche, the rest just jumped up and wrote their messages on the board. We hung the board in our main meeting room for the next two years as a constant reminder of our commitment.

Preparing to return home

The kick-off event was a success, and I think that was for three reasons. First, it was tailored to our particular challenges; it was not a generic design. Second, the group was the true extended leadership team of the business, not just a head office group. Third, and most important, we set an open and honest tone early in the programme and maintained it throughout.

We went from an atmosphere of "it's not safe to speak out here" to "it is very safe to speak because the only thing that matters is that we are going to crack these business issues".

No one thought for a second that what we had agreed to would be easy to achieve. We were going to ask our people, and ourselves, to think and act differently – to be open to new ways of working and to build an environment of trust and interdependence. It would be a challenge for our entire organization.

The Chairman's question – "Why are such talented people producing such mediocre results?" – had been replaying in my mind over the course of the event. But as we prepared to return home, I was excited and confident that we could turn this around. We had a clear and aligned agenda – an agenda I loved and a level of ambition I liked. It reflected a level of business behaviour that inspired me. I also felt that I now knew the team and that I had established my leadership. But I was worried as well – there was a lot of work to do and it was not a clean ship. But, we had made a good start.

Exceptional start to an exceptional relationship

James Hill
Chairman of Unilever Italy
www.unilever.com

As the recently appointed CEO of the UK ice cream and frozen food business, I was excited to attend my first major European meeting. After a day or two of routine presentations, speeches and new product introductions, the chairman of the conference announced to the assembled multitude, "Ladies and Gentlemen, there is someone I would like you all to meet." The room went quiet, the lights were turned low, the expectations were sky high – and then – a video! It was Kees, speaking from home about his sabbatical from Unilever, during which he had developed the FSHD Foundation to investigate, maybe even cure, his son's illness. This was just a preface to the announcement that, forthwith, Kees would assume responsibility for our European business becoming, among other things, my boss! I remember thinking that this was an exceptional event, done in an exceptional way, in an exceptional company. How else, in this demanding and competitive business world, could a man take an extended sabbatical, fight for a good cause and return with a huge promotion? I assumed that such a thing could only happen to an exceptional man – a man I subsequently came to know.

We signed up for the plan and the man

We've all been there, and it's easy enough to imagine … the senior management conference … the multi-day offsite … the diagonal slice … the PowerPoint presentations … the build-a-raft-from-matchsticks exercise … the flipcharts and Blu-Tak … the moments of inspiration … the moments of desperation! Ecoublay had all of that but with one difference, which made ALL the difference. On the final morning, unscripted yet meticulously prepared, Kees made a truly compelling state-of-the-union speech. Respect for the past, realism for the present, ambition for the future. The right combination of emotion and reason, strategy and tactics, fact and judgment. Turned out that the guy had been up all night – literally all night – to make sense of our collective ramblings of the previous two days. It was a winner, he was a winner, so possibly – just possibly – at long last, we could all be winners. I and all of my colleagues were happy to sign up, certainly for the plan, but also for the man.

The virtues of speed, accountability and cross-functional teamwork

It was my privilege and good fortune to become the first leader of SepCo (see SepCo box on page 80), a company within a company, an internal spin-off. Why me … the best man for the job, or the only man for the job? Would SepCo be a sick bay, or a departure lounge – a cash machine, or a mincing machine – not just for the brands, but also for the people in it? As senior as the sponsors were, the sceptics outnumbered the optimists. Well, against considerable odds, it actually worked! After three years, the portfolio's value was 50% greater than it was at the start. Profits went up, sales were up, morale was sky-high and important lessons were learnt, or re-learnt, about the virtues of speed, accountability and cross-functional teamwork in managing local brands. Unilever showed that it, too, could play the private equity game, and win. Of course, it is easy to appear clever with hindsight. The real credit goes to those with the vision and courage to set it up in the first place … none more than to Kees himself.

BREAKING PARADIGMS: REDUCING UNNECESSARY COMPLEXITY

By mid-2001, we had to face the fact that the profitability and market share of Unilever Europe's ice cream business were under pressure. The decline in some sectors was becoming a trend. Financial results were unpredictable due to the weather's impact on sales. People were even beginning to ask whether Unilever should stay in the ice cream business. Both overall profitability and the underlying sales figures were well below the Unilever average. Earlier that year in Ecoublay, we had formulated the MWBs for ICFE. Subsequently, the communications team did a great job of creating a figure that summarized everything from the vision to the scorecard (see Figure 1).

Senior managers from the organization were appointed to lead each of the five MWBs, in addition to their normal roles as country Chairmen. The progress of the take-home ice cream MWB was considered insufficient. The leadership of this MWB was struggling and even though the strategic intent was well formulated, it was not being translated into action. ICFE's leadership team concluded that a step change was necessary and that a concrete action plan was needed. We decided to assemble a multidisciplinary group of our most senior leaders to define a plan.

Preparation for the study tour

During a meeting at the Sheraton Hotel at Schiphol airport, a small project team, under my leadership, decided to profile a programme to address the issues facing the take-home MWB as a learning exercise. A week would be set aside for a study tour and the participants would be carefully selected to ensure that all the key players – key country leaders, functional leaders and a selection of high potential and influential managers – were present. The invitation would be personal, and it would come straight from me. It would be positioned as a must-attend workshop. At the Schiphol meeting, the team also defined the desired outcome of the study tour. An inspiring location was chosen on the Costa Brava, where we would meet in a lovely old hacienda.

Before leaving, we had to get the group in the right frame of mind. We decided

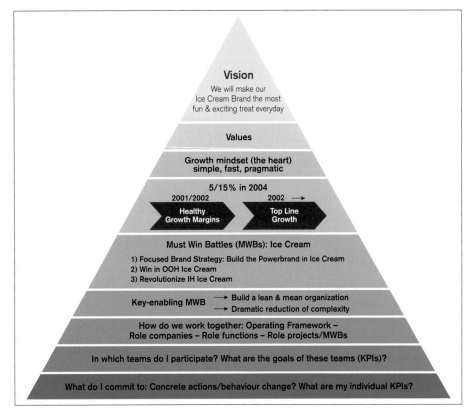

Figure 1: ICFE's Strategic Direction

to start with a mountain bike ride in the dunes of Santpoort, the Netherlands. This would create a bonding effect and it would provide an opportunity for me to make a powerful leadership call. The group would then return to Schiphol for a live link with the Chairman of Unilever's largest and most successful take-home ice cream business, Good Humor-Breyers in the US. Before departing in small groups to different countries in Europe for the fact-finding element of the programme, an ex Coca-Cola executive would give the group a lesson on how to conduct an effective store visit. At the end of the meeting, the project teams would get the go-ahead to begin the study tour.

The bike ride through the dunes of Santpoort

We arrived in Santpoort by train early in the morning. There was some excitement as to what was in store for the group. The weather was not great. Two lorries with mountain bikes and helmets were parked outside the station. I had done the track the previous week under the guidance of the organizers. Being experts in this kind of management outing, they advised me to chat with the participants a bit, but keep an eye on how everyone was doing. They suggested that once everyone seemed more or less ready, I get on my bike and start riding at a steady, fairly fast pace. They also recommended that somewhere, along the way I stop, walk away from my

bike, choose a position in a valley in the dunes and wait. I was to wait until everyone had gathered around me and stopped talking. At that moment, I could give them the brief for the rest of the week.

I was pretty sceptical about this. Would they follow me? Would they stop talking? Could I make myself heard? With all of these worries on my mind, I got on my bike without saying anything and started to ride. To my surprise, they got on their bikes and followed me. I kept a fairly fast pace. They kept following me. We left the main road, and took a small and winding sand path. There was no way to overtake me. A long, neat line of bikers continued to follow me. I could hear the heavy breathing of those following directly behind me. After 20 minutes of tough going, I stopped, got off my bike and walked down into a valley in the dunes. Everyone stopped and walked towards me. A few started to chat with me. At least they tried. I did not say anything. And indeed, they formed a circle around me and stopped talking. It felt like an hour before they finally quietened down. I addressed the team with a firm but low voice. Low enough that they had to group closer and listen intently to hear me. I explained the business issue and emphasized why they were here and why I had invited them and not anyone else. I told them that I had confidence that they would be able to solve the issue. I made it clear that dealing with this "burning platform" was a matter of urgency.

The first assignment was to find a quiet spot in the dunes and think about how they, as individuals, could make a difference in finding a solution for the problem. Everybody was given a small backpack containing a pen and a notebook so they could keep a record of all their observations.

Insights from Good Humor-Breyers

When we returned to the Sheraton, the group had their lesson on effective store visits. It was quite surprising to see that so many experienced managers actually learnt a few things (to put it mildly).

The video connection with Eric Walsh in Green Bay, Wisconsin, worked. He appeared on screen and gave a powerful lecture on the success factors of the Good Humor-Breyers (GHB) business. He challenged the team to copy the GHB model. The message was loud and clear – GHB had cracked this nut. What struck the team was the pragmatism, the simplicity and the emphasis on excellence in execution. The advertising executions were simple, straightforward messages that consistently positioned the brand for the consumer. It is also worth highlighting that Eric's leadership team had remained unchanged for more than five years – quite unusual for a Unilever operating company.

The deep dive

In total, over one and a half days, the groups visited:
- 5 countries
- 50 consumer homes
- 3 factories
- The head offices of 2 international customers (Tesco and Dia)
- 25 retail outlets
- 6 so-called benchmark companies (Danone, Heineken, Ben & Jerry's Europe, Coca-Cola)
- 3 qualitative consumer research firms
- 2 innovation centres of other categories (hair and margarine).

The deep dive in the market

The group was split into eight smaller multidisciplinary groups. The project team had constructed a marvellous schedule. Some groups were flying to other European countries, some stayed in the Netherlands, others were driving to Belgium and the north of France. Every group would visit the homes of one or two typical consumers and two or three retail outlets.

I was a member of the team that, among other things, visited the head offices of hard discounter Dia, a member of the Carrefour Group. We arrived early at their premises in Madrid. The local key account manager briefed us on what to expect, how to behave and asked us not to negotiate or give anything away. As good citizens, we entered the offices. The receptionist put us in a small, scruffy waiting room. There were not enough chairs and the ones that were available were very uncomfortable. We had to wait for 40 minutes before we were finally able to meet the person we were supposed to meet. He lectured for a while and complained about Frigo's lack of service. Finally, we got down to having a decent discussion about the ice cream business, the consumers and what they were looking for when buying ice cream at Dia. This gave us some good insight into the particular needs of a hard discounter – low price, special packaging, no out-of-stocks – and what we as a category leader had to do to get more shelf space.

Sharing the findings of the market dive

Everybody arrived more or less on time at the hacienda on the Costa Brava. Note that it was November – off-season in the Costa Brava. This was important because we were not there for a pleasant vacation. We were there because of the environment – it would help facilitate what we were trying to accomplish. Everyone seemed excited about the experience in the market. After we had dinner together, the groups prepared their presentations for the following morning. They were asked to present their comments in terms of the 4Cs (culture, consumer, customer and costs). The presentations were insightful.

The deep analysis of the 4Cs

Together the group made a list of the hard facts and issues in each area of the 4Cs. Breakout groups were formed and asked to study the insights and come forward with radical structural solutions. I made it very clear that I was not interested in politically correct answers. We had a big problem, which required us to challenge our actual ways of doing things. I also used the opportunity to remind the group that I was looking for "European" solutions, not "country" solutions.

Initial conclusions

Costs. We were way too expensive in both variable and fixed costs. We were suffering from complexity on all dimensions – products, processes, systems and structure.

Culture. The newly established Innovation Centre in Rome, which was supposed to do all the brand development for Europe, did not work. Its role was not accepted.

Consumer. Our brands were losing strength due to a lack of support and innovation. Viennetta (ice cream cake) was in real trouble.

Customer. There was a dramatic need to understand the individual requirements of different customers.

The impact of complexity

The impact of organizational complexity was brought out during one of the team's visits to a retail outlet. As one participant described: During a store visit, we found that there was a stocking problem with some of our products on the shelves. We asked to see the stock in the freezer as well as the stock on the shelves to understand where the problem lay – in the store itself or in our supply to the store. The store personnel reluctantly took our group back to the freezers, which were kept at temperatures well below zero – one of the worst jobs for any stocker was to have to go into these freezers. There, we saw a large supply of our products in the corners, all in identical looking boxes with small writing in the corner. To find the right flavour, a stocker would have to sort through all the boxes – in the freezing cold (-23° C)!

When we investigated further, we found that opening our boxes was one of the hardest jobs for a stocker – the super strong glue we used was almost impossible to open and regularly resulted in broken nails. In our drive to reduce costs through standardization, we had saved several hundred thousand euros a year by using standard brown boxes with small printing. In addition, we had once had a problem with boxes inadvertently opening, so the solution was to use the strongest glue available – no more problems with boxes breaking open, at least in transit. If we had not had people from supply chain, marketing and other areas there, no one would have believed this was a real problem. Sitting there altogether, we saw that well-intentioned decisions around the drive to reduce costs had led to an overambitious programme of harmonizing the size and colours of our outer cases, making them almost identical for the quick reader. By fixing one problem, we had created another, which resulted in our products not being available on the shelves.

The learning from this anecdote was that our marketers and product developers had to have an in-depth understanding of the needs of all the people in the total chain.

Every one to two hours, the groups came back to the plenary session to share conclusions and recommendations. The quality of the work differed dramatically by group. The consumer group was struggling; they were discussing their own interests and positions rather than the business issues. In the end, it was necessary to take one person out of the group and change the leader. Quite interestingly, the result was that this group went from debating to working closely with the cost/supply chain group. The culture group came up with good suggestions for the creation of a different mindset in the organization. More action; less debate. Good progress was also made in the customer area, with a call to focus on operational excellence. Or, as one of the members put it, we need to focus on the art of implementation.

Radical recommendations came from the cost group. Initially, there was some struggle in the plenary session with the nature of the advice. But after a few iterations, it became clear that the recommendations made sense. Their conclusion was that we were too complex in everything we did. Little incremental steps would not solve anything. The only way forward would be to make a few courageous management decisions and then to implement them with rigour and little debate. A hefty feeling of unease

The hard facts telling us we had a complexity issue

- 1,773 stock keeping units (SKUs) – with over 1,500 of these being sold in only one country.
- Only two countries had more standard European products than local-market-only products.
- Only one product was produced and sold in a common format across all markets (Magnum Almond).
- Over 400 scooping SKUs, over 300 cup SKUs and 19 SKUs of one single standard product (Cornetto Classico).
- Over 50 different vanilla mixes.
- 380 total suppliers.
- 1,070 mixes (recipes) with an average of 1.6 products per mix.
- Over 700 "different" flavours, with 35 strawberry flavours alone.

developed in the plenary discussion. Some participants were asking for more data, more research and work to take place before deciding. Others were arguing that the group in the room had all the power to make the decisions. They considered it our obligation as leaders to act – to act now and to act with determination.

I was pleasantly surprised by the group's recommendations. This was what I had hoped for. The group was taking its destiny in its own hands. The radical simplification measures that were being recommended made sense to me. If we were to implement the idea of a European product range, this would immediately move the ICFE business group from a loose federation of fairly independent companies to an integrated European business unit. This fit with the vision we had formulated in Ecoublay of our organizational structure. It would also empower the European board to make European decisions.

At the end of a long day, I invited the team to a special dinner in El Faro, a great restaurant on the coast. The project team had organized a surprise appearance of an authentic Flamenco dance group – not one of those touristy things, but the real thing. Everybody loved it, and it took the tension of the day's conclusions away. We had a great party, which was well deserved after all the hard work. I addressed the group during dinner, thanked them for their quality input and promised to reflect on it overnight and share my conclusions the following morning.

The summing up session
The next morning, I started by talking about the passion, energy and pride I saw in the Flamenco performance and how it was something we should also embrace. I then reiterated the point that the people in the room had been selected by me to be my leadership team. I trusted them and wanted them to take the space they needed to implement the agreed-upon actions. I expected them to fully lead the implementation and bring it to fruition on time and in accordance with the defined specifications. I told them that if they encountered difficulties, they should understand them, think them through, develop some alternatives and come forward with a recommendation. I asked them to stop delegating upwards; instead,

Flamenco dancers: Passion and energy

take the space that I was giving them and enjoy the journey. I then summarized the conclusions of the culture group. We agreed to stop rediscussing decisions, reinventing the wheel, second-guessing each other, having hidden agendas and finding excuses. We would strive for more trust, more teamwork and develop an

The Rubik Project

Reinier Kelder
Chief Procurement Officer
CSM NV
www.csmglobal.com

During his second week as president of the ICFE business group, Kees had an introductory meeting with the procurement team, where we showed him a few examples of how removing unnecessary complexity could achieve huge cost and agility benefits. Kees later told me that this meeting had been a real eye opener for him. Hence, the European ice cream business's game-changing complexity reduction program originated.

A taskforce was assembled with the overall aim of reducing the complexity of the entire portfolio to create space to grow the European ice cream business. I was the supply-chain member of a team of five high-potential individuals from finance, marketing and R&D. Jean-Marc Tilliard, the chairman of Frigo Spain and a Euroboard member was appointed as the task force leader. The project was called "Rubik", in recognition of the inventor of the cube that had one right solution that could be arrived at in myriad ways. Under Kees's leadership, we met with the other country chairmen to agree to and sign off on the program brief.

After nine months of very hard work, the project was successfully completed. Cost reductions of about €25 million in manufacturing and another €20 million in procurement were realized. Most importantly, there were almost no out-of-stocks, in what became one of the best summers of the century. Typically, we would have major out-of-stock problems in July during such a hot summer, but thanks to Rubik, the summer of 2003 resulted in record profits. Reflecting back seven years later, there are a few key learnings:

- **Courage and personal leadership.** Kees had a clear vision of what had to be achieved, and he created an environment in which the task force was truly empowered.
- **Country engagement.** Appointing the chairman of a big country as task force leader gave a clear signal that Rubik was a priority.
- **Top leadership commitment.** Kees was totally engaged and clear in every meeting and presentation to the business about the importance of Rubik.
- **A clear escalation mechanism.** The task force had full access to the Euroboard and progress was reviewed at every meeting as a standard agenda item. Any issue could be brought forward for top-level resolution, which was critical for making quick decisions.
- **Priority setting and focus.** All resources were focused on delivery of the Rubik project for nine months, including R&D, which was at the expense of innovation. This was a courageous decision, but one of the key enablers of success.
- **Risk management.** A transparent approval process was established for local country marketing directors to sign-off on product changes. If they disagreed, another set was produced for approval. If they still disagreed, the case was escalated to the Euroboard for a decision. In the end, we managed to reduce the product portfolio from about 1,800 to 835 within 12 months.

The concept of the European shopping basket

- All SKUs are by definition European.
- Each country can choose only from the European shopping basket.
- SKUs will be made available (on time, in full) with the right language.
- There will be a transparent transfer price system.
- 10% of the available SKUs will be value propositions.
- Marketing SVP becomes the gatekeeper of the brand development centre.
- Basket size is fixed at 800 SKUs.
- It will adhere to the principle of one SKU in, one SKU out.

attitude of relentlessly implementing what had been agreed to, rolling out proven successes, increasing our speed to market and having a simple and pragmatic mindset.

We agreed to reduce our complexity by 50%. This meant reducing raw materials, ingredients and packaging materials by half. And, we agreed that we would do this without any volume losses or deterioration in quality. A dedicated taskforce would be created and briefed within a week. The objective of the taskforce was to develop a European shopping basket of products that would be available to all countries with all languages on the packaging. We agreed to implement this for the 2003 season. The

leader of the task force would report directly to me and have full access to the European board. Every European board meeting would start with a review of this project.

Together with some other cost reduction measures, this would create room to put more advertising dollars behind the brands and, as a result, allow us to double our business in Europe over a period of five years.

Other agreed to measures included a 50% reduction in out-of-stocks, more effective but fewer promotions and the launch of good value-for-money products. Package designs had to improve in terms of shelf appeal, and space had to

insight

Keep in mind that complexity tends to creep back in – an empowered gatekeeper can play a critical role in ensuring that things don't go astray of the agreed upon objective.

be created for tailor-made products and promotions for large retail chains.

The elevator speech [5] read, "We had a great week. We were inspired by the rich outside inputs. We agreed to an action plan for our take-home business and we have a can-do mindset. We are committed to delivering and we will all play our part in making the plan happen. Implementing a radical plan to address complexity costs will be our focus area for 2002, and this will create the space and the resources for powerful product launches in 2003."

The group left the hacienda energized and ready to share the outcome with their teams.

The results

After several months of hard work, a European shopping basket of 835 products was defined. Every country could order from the basket. The packaging of the products was in all languages. Recipes met the legal requirements of all countries. Despite some

Achievement: The hard facts

	2001	2002
Number of SKUs	1,773	835
Number of ingredients	1,653	770
Number of packaging items:		
• Packaging materials	203	150
• Packaging dimensions	532	400
Number of suppliers	380	250

Under the Magnum Brand, 7 Deadly Sins – a limited edition series of ice cream flavours – was launched

IT problems, artwork was approved by all countries in time to meet the preproduction guidelines for the 2003 season. In 2003, the programme yielded €45 million in savings. That year also happened to have the best summer in the past 100 years. Out-of-stocks were kept within reasonable levels, thanks to the new way of managing the business. Despite R&D's focus on reducing complexity for nine months, they did manage to come up with one new line extension – Magnum 7 Deadly Sins – which proved to be a roaring success.

What was different and why it worked
- The **deep market dive** brought home, in a very convincing way, that we had a big – very big – problem with complexity, and SKUs were the root cause. There was full alignment on this. Everybody had experienced it. The design of the deep dive and the selection of the

companies and organizations that were visited were key.
- The group embraced an exceptional, even outrageous, target of reducing SKUs by 50%. No process other than this one could have generated the full acceptance of such an ambitious goal. It was **the group** that **proposed it**, and I was able to translate it into a commitment.
- Because all the key decision makers were part of the group that participated in the study tour, **we could make the decision on the spot**. We also impressed the organization with the aligned commitment and determination that we portrayed, and we surprised them with the speed at which we were able to form the taskforce, which consisted of first-class individuals from different functions.
- Every possible occasion was used within the organization to drive home

the message that, no matter what, the 50% reduction goal was going to be achieved! It was the **top priority for the business**. Nothing else was as important.

Side benefits of the project

- Common coding for all ingredients.
- European specifications for ingredients, packaging and products.
- Quality improvement.
- Increased speed to market.
- Active European portfolio management.
- Exploitation of new international logo.
- Improved responsiveness to market changes/demands in the supply chain.
- Improved line efficiencies.
- Reduction of start-up costs.
- Capital investment could be reduced by 30%.

Poul's Column

Simplifying the business to accelerate growth

Poul Weihrauch
President
Wrigley Europe – www.wrigley.com

Wrigley, the world's leading chewing gum company, was acquired by Mars Inc. in October 2008 for $23 billion. In March 2009, Wrigley's European Management team came together under new leadership to craft a growth strategy in the midst of the economic crisis and develop cross-functional high performance team behaviours.

The challenge facing us was clear. Many small stores closed during the crisis and this had impacted our sales. In addition, our European business was complex – we supplied 30 countries from four factories, which made the job of the factories increasingly difficult. We manufactured more than 2,000 SKUs in Europe and our working capital was high to service our customers.

During a Wrigley management team meeting, Kees shared his story of Unilever's European ice cream business – ironically, a competitor to Mars ice cream. The Defining Moment for us was when Kees said that Unilever had space for only 16 to 24 variants of ice cream in a freezer, but the markets had 36 on the impulse ice cream price card. Suddenly we realized that our gum display rack was the equivalent of Unilever's freezer cabinet. While we could have between 20 and 50 SKUs, some countries had 3 to 4 times that in SKUs. Thus, we embarked on a year-long "Fuel for Growth" programme to simplify our portfolio and reinvest the benefits into business growth activities.

As a result, we reduced our SKUs by 30%, our gum formulas by 42% (with improved product quality) and our configurations (palletisation) by 50%. Not only did the programme reduce complexity, but it also improved our customer service levels and reduced working capital. All gains were reinvested in consumer advertising to the benefit of our business and our customers.

Who would have thought that a freezer of ice cream could inspire a chewing gum company to higher performance?

A Subsidiary of Mars, Incorporated

THE DAY OF MY BOARD APPOINTMENT: FROM DREAM TO NIGHTMARE

As President of the Ice Cream and Frozen Foods Europe business group, I reported to the President of Global Ice Cream, Rob Polet, along with a few functional Senior Vice Presidents (SVPs) and regional leaders for North America and the Developing and Emerging Markets. Rob was a member of the Foods Executive, the management team responsible for the Foods Division, led by Patrick Cescau (see Appendix II). This was an ideal situation for me. Rob, who I knew well and liked, was a great boss. He gave a lot of freedom, but he also stimulated and inspired people to go the extra mile, and he kept the nonsense and politics of the Foods Division at bay. This enabled me to focus on the task of building a strong, high-performing team. Once every two months I had a coaching session with Patrick.

The other members of Patrick's Foods Division team were the regional Presidents of Europe, Asia, North America, Latin America and Africa/Middle East. The President of Foodsolutions, Unilever's foodservice business, as well as a Marketing President, and the SVPs for sales, supply chain, HR and finance also reported to Patrick (see Appendix I). Most Presidents and SVPs were talented and ambitious individuals. As members of the Foods Executive, they had monthly meetings and spent a lot of their time on

the integration of the Bestfoods business, which Unilever had acquired in 2000. Growth was another of their key worries.

In Almeria, where I had my true leadership moment, Antony Burgmans and Patrick Cescau (the Unilever Co-chairmen) probably decided that I could be a candidate for the Unilever Board and the Unilever Executive. A few months later, in early 2003, Antony invited me to his office, where he asked me how I would react if I were asked to join the board. I was stunned. It had never occurred to me that I was a crown prince. I had my ice cream job. And, yes, I delivered some nice results, but

I was in a position that was a full layer away from the Unilever Executive and Board. All the members of the Foods Division and Home and Personal Care Division were, in my mind, ahead of me in the running. When I tried to get Antony to explain, he made it very clear that this was not my concern. He also made it clear that he was just asking if I would be interested if the Nomination Committee of the board were to ask me. Absolutely nothing was being offered at this moment in time. He was only sounding me out. I just had to answer the question. He said I could discuss it with Renée that evening because this appointment would make me a public person; my privacy would be reduced and I would be carrying an enormous responsibility on my shoulders. He stressed that if I mentioned the conversation to anyone else except Renée, I would not make it to the board. Totally baffled, I left his office.

That evening, Renée and I discussed it over a glass of wine. This was so unexpected and it was such an honour – the crowning achievement of my career – so, rather than talk about the implications and consequences, we talked more about the surprise factor, who else would be asked and who was leaving the board. It was clear to both of us that the answer I would give Antony would be a firm YES.

When I informed Antony about our decision, he repeated the warnings about confidentiality and the fact that the board still had to go through the normal evaluation process. He explained the process in a few sentences – long list, short list, preferred candidate, board decision – and said that it could take a while. His advice was to forget the conversation and concentrate on my job. Easier said than done. It was always in the back of my mind, and I was always trying to read messages into the behaviour of individuals, but I never mentioned it to anyone. Time passed.

In February 2004, all of Unilever's senior managers were attending the OBJ event, which stands for "Oh be joyful". This event, which is full of traditions, brings together 200 of Unilever's senior leadership team to listen to the two Chairmen present the annual results and the outlook for the future. It is followed by a black-tie dinner. There were many important undertones associated with the OBJ: Who would be invited to sit at each board member's table? Who would be asked to reply to the speech of one of the Chairmen? Often, this person was next in line for the board.

I actually enjoyed the OBJ and its traditions. It was a great occasion to see many old friends and to do a bit of business on the sidelines. That evening, if I remember correctly, I was, seated at Patrick's table. I was not asked to be a speaker. During the results presentation, Niall FitzGerald, one of the Co-chairmen, announced that he would be retiring from the Unilever Board and the Executive at the next shareholders' meeting in May. It

was also announced that Unilever would move towards a "real" one-tier supervisory board. In other words, important decisions had been made and the key steps were being shared with the senior leadership in complete confidence. During dinner, we talked about Niall's retirement and the fact that Unilever would be moving to a one-tier supervisory board.

At the end of the dinner, Antony asked me to join him in the car back to Wassenaar, the village where we both lived. So, here we were, in the back of a car, in the dark, unable to look each other in the eye, and Antony tells me that the board had voted in my favour. It was all pretty surreal. My reaction must have seemed utterly stupid. I whispered something like, "Thanks for the confidence". Almost in the same breath, he went on to tell me that the next morning – actually that day, as it was already well past midnight – at 8 am, an announcement would be made to the stock exchanges and the press that Niall was retiring, that Patrick would become the Co-chair succeeding Niall, I would succeed Patrick on the Unilever Executive as Director of the Foods Division and that I would join the board. I could not believe it. All of a sudden, a dream I never felt possible had come true.

Strangely enough, my first thought was of my father. He had passed away in 1980. As a former Director of the Nationale Nederlanden Insurance Company, he had always wanted me to be successful in my

career. How proud he would have been. I could envision him jumping for joy on top of his beautiful cloud in the sky. The next thought was one of being overwhelmed by the responsibility of leading a division, which was more than half the size of Unilever. A few seconds later, I came back to Earth, back to the reality of sitting in the back of a car in the dark of night, having just been told by the Chairman that I had made it to the top.

I asked a few operational questions about what was going to happen the next day. It was immediately clear that this was not the time to be pragmatic. Antony's response was, "Tomorrow, Patrick's Foods Executive meeting starts at 9 am. Just be there and agree to a good handover plan with them." Full stop. The car had pulled into my driveway. I got out, and there I was, all alone with my thoughts and my excitement. I could not wait to tell Renée that I was going to be the Director of the Foods Division. Of course, she was already in bed. This was probably the only time that I did not sneak into bed, trying not to wake her up. Lights on, I told her everything that had happened. We just tried to imagine what was going to happen tomorrow. We made a list of family and our dearest friends who we wanted reach before the news reached them. I also wanted to inform my team before they heard it on the wire. And then there was Mike, my driver, and Lisette, my assistant. It was clear that I had to get up very early the next morning to make all the phone calls and get an e-mail out to all my direct reports. That night, I slept really well, oblivious to what was going to happen a few hours later.

The day of the announcement
The announcement of changes at the top of Unilever was considered price sensitive information. This means that the board is obliged, according to the law, to inform the stock exchanges of any changes at the earliest moment after a decision has been made. As the Unilever Board had reached its conclusion after the markets had closed, the first opportunity was early the next morning. Both the press office and the investor relations department were very eager to do a first-class job. The profit-warning announcement a few months earlier had not been well handled, and it had led to a significant drop in our share price. Now the communication process had to be handled very carefully.

The announcement went out early and the newswires picked it up very quickly. They insisted on immediate interviews with both Antony and Patrick. Of course, both were well prepared, but the sheer number of interviews did not give them time to pay attention to the internal communication, most importantly, Patrick's direct reports – the members of the Foods Executive – would soon become my subordinates. They either heard the news when they arrived at the office or on the way into

> **insight**
>
> *Communication cannot be an afterthought or done on the fly. Every time you or your team have reached a conclusion, you must design the communication process. Any meeting that does not finish with a discussion and agreement on the key messages – who will deliver them and how – is a bad meeting.*

the office. Probably four or five of them thought that they would be next in line to lead the Foods Division.

In the meantime, the atmosphere on the Ice Cream and Frozen Foods Europe floor was quite different. The telephones were ringing and people gathered around my desk to share in the excitement. Everybody was really nice, positive and complementary. I was so proud and pleased. I had been able to beat the newswires with my message to the Ice Cream team. My key family members had been informed, and I was ready to go to the top floor for the Foods Executive meeting.

A few minutes before the kick-off, Mary, Patrick's assistant, called to inform me that Patrick was completely tied up in press interviews and would not be able to come to the meeting for the next hour or so. "OK", I thought, "I had better go to the meeting and show my face." In high spirits, I went to the boardroom on the tenth floor where the Foods Executive meeting was

supposed to take place. I walked into the room and noticed that several groups were standing in corners in heated debates. I went around and received ice-cold "congratulations" from most of the people. I felt horrible. I clearly was not welcome; I was the wrong person, in the wrong place, at the wrong time. It became clear to me that Patrick had not been able to inform all his team members before the announcement, which on its own caused some irritation. On top of that, there was the injustice of it all – someone who was not even a member of the Foods Executive, but a subordinate of one of them, was going to be the new boss of the division. Of course, these were all very normal human reactions. But, for me, my dream has just turned into a nightmare.

Sandy Ogg, the Senior Vice President of HR for the Foods Division, took the initiative to get everyone to sit down. I took a seat, and before I realized what was happening, everyone was sitting as far away from me as possible. I was isolated from them. I had become public enemy number one, and they were closing ranks on me to show their strength. Sandy pointed out that this was no way to welcome the new leader. Immediately, the frustrations started to flare. Sandy decided to stop the meeting – the right decision. He also invited all the Foods Executive members to come to his office individually to have an open and private conversation – another good decision. He promised he would listen very carefully and come back to the Executive, particularly to Patrick and me, with a proposal on how to deal with the current situation. The rest of that day and the following week, Sandy spoke to everyone.

What an awful start to the first day after the announcement of my appointment.

The hurt feelings quickly disappeared when I returned to my office to find many e-mails and telephone messages congratulating me on my appointment. At home, Renée became part of the pleasant experience, as she also received many lovely messages and flowers, which she loves.

The on-boarding process

Sandy kept me constantly in the loop about his conversations, and he shared some general insights with me, without breaking the confidentiality agreement he had with the individuals. He prepared a list of general issues and a list of people who might reconsider their position with Unilever and decide to leave the business for an outside position.

The list of general issues included some easy points to address, such as: Who is Kees? What has he achieved? How does he want to work? The more difficult question was, "Why was Kees chosen and

not me?" The list of those who might leave the company was worryingly long. Sandy and I agreed that a process was needed to get me fully introduced to the team, before taking over from Patrick in May. I asked him to think about that and to come forward with a recommendation.

His idea was, to put it mildly, unusual and not without risk. He proposed that we organize a session for all the team members the evening before the next Foods Executive meeting. The purpose of the session would be to help me relate to the team by positioning me properly and addressing all the misconceptions

and stories that were flying around about me and my leadership style. Furthermore, he suggested that Patrick should not be there and that he should not interfere with the approach. As I now felt comfortable sharing some deeper insights about myself, I quickly embraced Sandy's idea.

The first part of the session involved me sharing my lifeline (opening myself up in a very personal way) with the team. The first time I did this was in Ecoublay when I was appointed as President of the Ice Cream and Frozen Foods Europe in 2001. It had been well received then, so I thought why not do it again. We held the session in front of the fireplace in the board dining room at Unilever's Rotterdam offices. In hindsight, we could have chosen a better, more informal location. But it was convenient and acceptable. I spoke to the team for about half an hour, sharing my motives, beliefs, drivers, values and behaviours. I also spoke about my family and the FSHD Foundation.

Then I was asked to leave the room, while they discussed, under Sandy's leadership, what else they wanted to know about me. Sandy orchestrated it in such a way, that the discussion went from topic to topic. At the end of the discussion, Sandy's right hand, Guy de Herde, brought me a list of questions, and he added a bit of colour to the questions so that I could get a good feel for what was going on in the other room. When the team had exhausted their discussions, they broke for a while to give me a chance to prepare my responses.

I tried to be as honest, truthful and authentic as possible. When I re-entered the board dining room, I could already feel a different atmosphere from when we had started the session. I took my time, answered each question and addressed every issue that was raised. They listened intently to my answers. At the end, I asked if I had responded to all their questions

Unilever Board – 2004

and if my responses had raised any further questions. A few additional questions were asked, but nothing material came up.

Sandy rounded the session off by giving a summary and asking the members of the Foods Executive team, one by one, if they were clear about me as their future leader and if they were confident that there was sufficient mutual ground for the development of a fruitful cooperation between the team and their boss. In the end, they all agreed that it had been wrong to offload their anger and frustration about the communication process on me. After some spontaneous and real handshaking and hugging, the wine bottles were opened, and we sat in a small circle drinking quite a few glasses of wine and toasting the great future of the Foods Division with their new leader.

> **insight**
>
> *An essential element of communication is repetition – messages are only heard and digested when they are repeated in a consistent and compelling way over and over again.*

I went home, really pleased with the good atmosphere that had been created thanks to a well thought through, but risky, on-boarding process. That night I dreamt again. The nightmare was history.

Observations

- **Communication in this particular story:** The communication in this case was completely dominated by the corporate governance rules and practices. The financial market authorities have set rules that are so tight that the board of a public company is limited in what it can or cannot say, and more precisely, when it can release messages related to so-called price sensitive information. It is up to the judgment of the board and its legal counsel what information is considered price sensitive. In today's world, it is not surprising that boards are inclined to take a prudent approach and qualify certain decisions as price sensitive more often than not. There is no doubt that the announcement about the board changes was price sensitive and therefore the rules of the stock

market needed to be followed. However, despite the rules and regulations, one should always respect the feelings of the key individuals. Even if it is late in the day or evening, a leader should ensure that those people personally affected by a decision hear the news directly from the boss, in person or by phone, and not from the news media. In today's world, with e-mail and text messages, it requires little effort to prepare messages that will go out to individuals at a pre-determined time. And nowadays, everyone is connected 24/7 through iPhones and BlackBerry devices for example. Like it or not, it's today's reality.

- **Trust:** I am convinced that it is possible to share confidential information with a member of your team. You should be able to trust the individual not to breach confidentiality. If that is not the case, then that individual should not be part of your team or your organization. A little more trust in our dealings with each other would create a much more pleasant and productive business climate.

UNILEVER EUROPE: HOW I BUILT THE TEAM

In March 2005, after becoming the President of Unilever Europe, my biggest challenge was to keep what little momentum there was in the business and not paralyze sales with too many organizational changes. The organization's design had to be dynamic, and because of the restructuring that had taken place, it had to initially respect the fact that we had to bring together three different European business groups, with different business systems, different cultures and different histories. At the same time, I had to find a solution for bringing together three operating companies at the country level. I needed the best, I needed them motivated and I needed them fast – as of April 1, 2005.

After mapping out the organizational structure and identifying the line-up of individuals I wanted to fill the slots, I went to see Patrick and Sandy. I was prepared for a long and intense meeting. The reality was different. Patrick started by stating that I had first choice for selecting my team because I was facing the toughest job in Unilever. He understood and accepted the top structure I had developed. The dynamic nature of it was clear to him. As far as people were concerned, both Sandy and Patrick were impressed with the team I had identified. I was only challenged in one area – finance – but we quickly reached a decision on the best possible candidate.

I left Patrick's office excited. I felt really supported, and there was real recognition of the fact that this was going to be a fierce challenge. I decided to move swiftly. The conversations with the selected individuals went smoothly. Everybody was on board. There was some discontent with the job titles as some people with the title "President" would now become "Executive Vice President." My argument is always simple. If you like the job, the prospects and the salary, take the job and do not argue about the title.

Nobody outside Unilever understands our titles anyway!

I first met Annie McKee (founder of the Teleos Leadership Institute) together with Tom Malnight after the leadership journey in Costa Rica that Niall FitzGerald and Antony Burgmans had organized in 2001 for their top 120. Smaller leadership journeys were subsequently set up for all the business groups in Ecoublay. I had been deeply impressed with the program and the role Tom and Annie played, so it was no surprise that I contacted them to share the changes at Unilever and the new challenges that I had been offered.

Unilever Executive – 2005

Why do talented people produce mediocre results?

Annie McKee
Founder
Teleos Leadership Institute – www.teleosleaders.com

We see it all the time – good people who just can't seem to do better than average. They're average performers, average managers and worst of all, they're average leaders. They're smart. They're committed (or at least they start out that way). They *want* to do a good job. So why do they produce mediocre results?

Kees van der Graaf's experience – and a hefty dose of neuroscience – can help us to understand the answer to this question. Constant pressure, small and large crises at work and the inevitable highs and lows of life can, over time, cause us to experience *power stress* – a state of chronic and unhealthy tension that affects our ability to think, reason and live whole and healthy lives. This isn't just a psychological state – it's a physiological state. The neurological effects of power stress include impaired cognitive functioning, which in turn leads to poor decisions and underperformance.

When we fall prey to power stress, we also lose sight of the importance of mindfully attending to ourselves as *whole people* – mind, body, heart and spirit. To be at our very best, we need to consciously focus on developing our minds – learning, expanding our horizons and honing our cognitive abilities. Our brains need to grow to keep up with our fast-changing world. We literally need to create new neural pathways to support new ways of behaving and leading.

We also need to attend to our physical well-being – basic needs such as water, good food and rest can make a huge difference in how we feel, how clearly we think and how others experience us.

For our relationships and emotional lives, we need to develop emotional intelligence – self-awareness, self-management, social awareness and relationship management. Emotional intelligence is at the heart of great performance at work and in life – the research is clear and common sense backs it up. To get things done right, we need to understand ourselves, have empathy for others and have strong, healthy relationships. We need to be able to inspire and motivate people – even people who are very different from ourselves. We need to use emotion wisely – which doesn't always mean being "nice". Emotionally intelligent leaders understand and manage their emotions, as well as the emotions and moods of others – just as Kees did when he became aware of and used his own feelings about his team and his business. *This is what differentiates outstanding leaders*.

Maybe most importantly, we need to attend to our spirit – the essential beliefs and values that guide us and give us the courage to do the right thing. At the heart of all great work (and great results) is our noble purpose. Kees van der Graaf's life is guided by his noble purpose.

Talented people have no business producing mediocre results, and they don't have to. It's up to each of us to minimize the impact of power stress. We need to take care of it before it takes care of us. And we need to attend mindfully to ourselves as full and complete human beings. The people whom we serve deserve the very best we can give.

TELEOS LEADERSHIP INSTITUTE

They immediately offered to support me in designing a roadmap to energize and prepare the new European leadership team for its mammoth task.

All three of us strongly believed in bringing a new team together in an inspiring environment as early as possible. As the members of the new team were going to start in their new roles on April 1, I wanted to bring them together in the second half of March for at least three or four days. All players had to make themselves available and had to be present without exception. Those who had previously worked with me, did not need any convincing. They had already seen the impact of such a teambuilding event. Some of the newcomers had to be given some subtle encouragement. And in the end, everyone turned up.

Four Acres: The teambuilding event

The venue was Unilever's training centre, Four Acres at Kingston upon Thames. It is a lovely, stately old home situated in the forest with fantastic facilities for group exercises, plenary discussions and syndicate work. But more importantly, it was an iconic venue at the time. Whenever you went to Four Acres for a general management course, you knew that your career was progressing nicely.

We had spent quite a few days designing the program. The objectives were twofold. First, we had to lay the foundation for a truly effective team. As I have explained, I believe that real teams can perform miracles. They are much better than the sum of the individuals. They help each other, they support each other, they build upon each other's ideas and most importantly, they trust each other. Second, we had to list the issues, prioritize them and formulate our business agenda for the rest of the year.

insight

Real teams are much better than the sum of the individuals. They help each other, they support each other, they build upon each other's ideas and most importantly, they trust each other.

We agreed to do a few exercises in order to get to know each other and to understand each other's motives and drivers.

- **Conversations with colleagues.** During the first evening, each team member had to have a personal conversation with at least two others, covering topics such as their hopes and how they expected their relationships to evolve.
- **The shock factor.** I asked the team members to list the most important unthinkable changes that had happened and what would give them hope for the future. This gave us a good feel for what was going on in their minds.
- **How did I get here?** Each of the 14 people involved were asked to give a personal reflection on the journey that had led to them now being part of this team including, for example: What are you most proud of? What have you learnt about yourself? What do you want to leave behind? What do you want to achieve? The discussion that followed started to create the team.
- **Dreams and fears of the new matrix structure.** We may not have chosen this new structure, but we are now responsible for making it work. The participants were asked to identify the critical interfaces and the kinds of behaviour that would be required. The following discussion allowed us to list the acceptable and unacceptable behaviours and to identify some of the weak points in the operating framework.
- **Our team charter.** This exercise involved discussing the wishes for the team and how we would work together as team mates.
- **Message to Kees.** Each team member listed their expectations of me as their leader. I received a number of very useful messages.
- **My leadership manifesto.** Each individual had to take a good hour to prepare their own leadership manifesto, answering questions like: How can we become resonant with each other and create resonance in Unilever Europe through our leadership? How will we connect with people's hearts?

All of these inputs and the conclusions of each session were carefully documented. The idea was to create a living document that would guide us through the years to come. At regular intervals, we would review our progress against the agreements we reached at Four Acres. In one of my last speeches to the team, I reflected on the powerful commitments we had each made and,t more importantly, on the fact that we had all lived up to our commitments.

Besides the softer side of creating a real team, we also agreed on the jobs that needed to be done:

- Stop the volume decline before the end of the year, through a mixture of short-term measures. Focus on the core products of our portfolio. No fancy launches, but make our existing successful products even more successful. Stop the flood of useless promotions.
- Implement the one-Unilever organization within 18–24 months in all countries. Investigate what lessons could be learnt from the Nordic structure. (Could we extract more value from our operations by combining a few country operations into one multi-country organization?)
- Close the old Home and Personal Care (HPC) office in Brussels before the end of the year.
- Agree to the proposed organizational structures for each country and function and identify the candidates for these jobs within a month.

- Reach a decision for project Mountain (the creation of one supply chain company for Europe) by October.
- Appoint the suppliers for the outsourcing of HR and Finance shared services in the coming months.
- Investigate the options for the creation of one ERP (enterprise resource planning) system for the entire European organization.

Most importantly, in my opinion, was the decision to visit all of our operations in pairs in the first week of April. It meant a huge sacrifice for everybody. Within a few days, we all had to empty our diaries to create the time to visit three to four counties in four days. Identical presentations were prepared for all countries. We decided to follow the same format in every country – first a meeting with the National Chairman, then a meeting with the leaders of the existing operations, then a meeting with the boards of the companies, followed by a presentation to all managers with a question and answer session at the end of the presentation. Before the departure to the airport, there would be a one-on-one meeting with the local Chairman and one of my team members.

We agreed which pairs would visit which countries. At the end of each day, the pairs would share their experience with our VP Communications who would be travelling with me and who would compile and improve the presentation for the countries. On Friday afternoon, after

the last day of the trip, there would be a conference call with all the managers in the region to confirm our change agenda for the coming year.

The decision to go on the country tour created an enormous amount of energy in the team. We were going to establish our leadership in an impactful and unconventional way. Never in the history of Unilever had this been done before. This was going to send a huge signal throughout the organization. We could not have thought of a better wake-up call.

I left Four Acres exhausted, but incredibly satisfied. I was so pleased with my line-up. With this team, I felt I could conquer the world, or better said, bring Unilever Europe back to where it ought to be – delivering sustainable results, meeting its targets.

By the end of the year, we had managed to stop the decline in volume.

MY SLEEPLESS NIGHT: LAYING THE FOUNDATION FOR A NEW PLAN

Though we achieved all our targets in 2005, it had been a challenging year. Competition was intensifying, and the retail trade was becoming more aggressive every day. Hard discounters were growing rapidly and putting a lot of price pressure on the markets. Our internal operating framework was good from a design perspective, but the category organizations, which were responsible for the delivery of relevant innovation and strong communication, were not delivering what Europe needed. On top of that, we had too many factories and our overheads were far too high. In that context, we were not growing fast enough, and our profitability was not good enough. The status quo was no longer an option; we needed to come up with a way to not only survive but also thrive in the current environment.

> **insight**
>
> *Have regular – at least once a year – moments of reflection with your team. This works best away from the office.*

The IMD retreat: Reflecting on the current reality

In order to reflect on the challenges we were facing in 2006, analyse the current reality and prepare the groundwork for 2007's plans and budget, I organized a week-long retreat for Unilever Europe's leadership team in the summer of 2006, after a year and a half in my role as President of Europe. The retreat was held at IMD's campus in Lausanne, Switzerland. The team included the five Chairmen of the largest European country operations, the functional heads, and the Senior VP responsible for the European supply chain company.

Professor Tom Malnight served as the facilitator; he not only organized a great programme but was also able to get the best lecture room on the top floor of IMD's Learning Centre, with stunning views of Lake Geneva and the Alps. It created a very inspirational setting. Our hotel was in the small medieval village of Lutry, which sits nestled between the shores of Lake Geneva and the Lavaux vineyards. Every morning we travelled by boat to IMD's campus, which provided us with an ideal way to start the day in an informal setting and get ready for a couple of hours of deep thought. During each session, we were challenged by several faculty members as well as by one another, which culminated in some intense but constructive conflicts and discussions.

IMD campus, Lausanne, Switzerland

Lavaux vinyards on the shores of Lake Geneva

The defining moment came when Lord David Simon, the senior independent director on the non-executive Board of Unilever and the previous CEO of BP, joined us. Although it was an unusual thing to do in those days, I invited him because I had got to know him well through our membership on Unilever's Board, and I was deeply impressed by his wisdom. Not only did he accept my invitation but he also gave us a full day of his precious time. During his introduction, he gave us some insights into the lessons he had learnt when he was responsible for BP's European business, and he bridged his experiences with Unilever Europe. After a great Q&A session, he left behind a group that was highly positive, motivated and ready for action.

By the end of the week, the team had concluded that we were going to face even bigger challenges in the near future. They determined that their leader (me!) should use the quieter summer months to reflect upon all of the outcomes during the week and present conclusions and recommendations for a sustainable solution to the team at the end of August.

It is important to note that the team did not delegate this problem upward, leaving me with the dirty task of solving the unsolvable. This was not at all the case. It was the result of five days of intense debates, and together we looked at all the issues from many different angles. We had created a clear picture of the current reality, and we had a good list of priorities

and actions. The team would address all the short-term actions that were required to get Unilever Europe ready for 2007. I was asked to use the summer to think long and hard about a longer-term plan to address the issues we would be facing in the future. The plan needed to be along the lines of the shared view developed at IMD. I loved it because it released me from dealing with the short-term issues and allowed me to focus on the long term with a small team around me.

Unilever's strategic planning process

With the help of some consultants, the really clever people in Unilever's strategy group had designed a process to develop a strategic plan for the next three to five years. It divided the Unilever world into the 12 categories in which it operated globally (skincare, laundry, household cleaners, savoury products, ice cream, spreads and so on). It also divided the world into a number of geographic regions. A region could be a large country (e.g. Germany, UK, France, China, India, US, Russia) or a sub-region (e.g. Middle East, Southeast Asia, Eastern Europe, Central America). In total, there were some 25 different "regions". If one put the categories and regions into a matrix, there were around 300 cells.

The first and second rounds

As a first step, the category teams were asked to put together a plan for each category with clear recommendations for

Lord Simon's Column

The European challenge

Lord Simon of Highbury

To be a non-executive member of a Board in a huge multinational like Unilever is somewhere between being a "football trainer" and a "plain clothes policeman". A football trainer because you are not going to kick the ball in earnest again but you think you know how you would; a cop because you have to look out to see things in the company are on the right road.

When I first met Kees, I thought he was a dedicated, serious and kind man: I worried at Board meetings that turning the Unilever European business around to adequate profit would put too much strain on him. He would not be able to cut through the protective layers of the Unilever organization to fundamentally reshape the asset base. Too many jobs were at risk, too many plants needed to be closed and Europe was the sentimental heart of the business. He would have a good shot at it; but he would compromise and come up short. He was too kind.

When Kees asked me to his retreat in Lausanne to discuss the need for change with his team, I was pleased. The football trainer in me wanted to see Kees's team in action. I thought I should be very frank and direct about my BP experience a decade or so earlier when we had totally reorganized our European structure.

Watching Kees with his team convinced me he had a chance to pull off a really significant business transformation. He was authentic and honest during that day. He did not quibble, nor hide. His team was not united – they were open and tough.

That day persuaded me to back Kees at the coming series of Board meetings. His strong values and personal commitment made the prospect of a business transformation a serious one. I made a positive judgment about his values and his stamina. These are crucial elements. Those who have the right ones deserve support. But the mindset of the team is also a critical factor. His team was up for a challenge: ready for leadership and full of ideas, which created positive energy. It would need a thoughtful, listening and determined leader.

The European experience for Unilever, which Kees faced, seemed daunting for Unilever; in truth, it was only the first and measured step in the massive changes that globalization would bring to Western-based businesses.

the different sub-regions. The Unilever Executive, which was responsible for managing profit and loss and delivering growth across regions, categories and functions, then discussed these inputs at a three-day session and found that they did not meet expectations. The Executive gave the category teams some strong but clear feedback and decided that round two should focus only on those cells in which Unilever had a turnover of more than €100 million. It also decided that the strategic role for each of those €100 million cells should be defined, as follows:

- Grow market share
- Maintain market share
- Manage for cash.

This seemed like a simple but clear way to define the criteria for resource allocation. If the objective was to grow market share, then more cash would have to be invested, and this cash would come from those cells designated "manage for cash".

As a result of the second round, the Unilever Executive now found itself having to deal with the issue of too many "grow market share" cells and not enough "maintain market share" and "manage for cash" cells. New criteria were formulated, and the category teams redid their homework.

The final round

Both the category teams and the Unilever strategy team did brilliant preparation work. Meetings among the country regional marketers and global category teams had taken place to discuss all the important cells prior to the next Unilever Executive meeting. At this meeting, the Executive was able to find solutions to all of the unresolved issues, and the financial group was happy because the plan would more than meet the expectations of the financial markets. Since we still had some meeting time left, an eager and clever function head suggested we do a risk assessment, which we considered a great idea.

In doing this, we rated each cell based on the following qualifications:

• The level of risk is high, medium or low
• The risk is manageable: yes, perhaps or no.

In record time, we attached a risk assessment to each of the almost 200 cells we discussed in the meeting. All of us left the meeting totally satisfied with the process, the outcome and the fact that year one of the strategic plan would now form the basis for our 2007 annual budget.

The alarm goes off

The Unilever Executive meetings took place in the London offices, and the following day, there would be another meeting focused on the operational side of the business. As usual, I slept in the Crowne Plaza Hotel next door to Unilever House. If I was lucky, I would get a room that was literally eight metres away from my office at Unilever. It was so close that I could check on the cleaning staff. So much for creating a little distance between your work and personal life. I went to my room and ordered a hamburger with room service; I hate sitting in a restaurant by myself, waiting for the food to come and either reading or staring at all the people having fun with their friends. Also, I knew there would be a heap of e-mails waiting for me.

Even though I had left the meeting earlier in the day feeling totally satisfied, I began to sense that something was wrong. I could not understand why I was beginning to feel uncomfortable. Perhaps it was because I had already begun to reflect on the longer-term issues facing the European business. It had been a great, highly effective meeting but something was not right. The feeling was getting stronger and stronger, so I took out my notes from the meeting and started to list all the cells in the European business group's countries and sub-regions. For each country, I listed the strategic role and the risk assessment. Next, I summarized each of the 12 categories for Europe. Of course, this was a little bit of a weighted average done on the back of an envelope.

The resulting picture was a real shock for me. Most categories were qualified as "maintain market share" or "manage for cash". Given the situation in Western Europe, this was not a surprise. In the Eastern European countries, the picture was different. There we had a large number of "grow market share" cells, but the real issue was the risk qualification. With the exception of ice cream, all the other 11 categories were qualified as high risk, but just manageable. Looking at that picture, I could only reach one logical conclusion. Eleven times high risk that was just manageable could mean only one thing – it was unmanageable!

So there I was, sitting alone in my hotel room facing a crisis. At that point, I made a conscious decision to start addressing the issue without involving anyone from my team. After playing with the numbers, I decided that there was only one conclusion – a radical solution was necessary. Hours later an alternative plan started to emerge. Paper was strewn about everywhere in my room. Time did not matter anymore. The only thing that mattered was creating a realistic plan for the future of Unilever Europe. For the last two years, we had been merely hanging in, making our targets through clever financial engineering. This situation was clearly not sustainable.

At around 6 o'clock in the morning, I finished the new plan. As I am absolutely incapable of putting anything into a PowerPoint presentation, I wrote a one-page summary by hand. I decided to go immediately to Unilever House and position myself in front of Patrick Cescau's office. I knew he would be in early, and I wanted to speak to him before the Unilever Executive meeting started again. Indeed, he did arrive early, and it was obvious from the way I looked that something big was bothering me. He invited me into his office, and I started to talk. I took him through my conclusions from the strategic plan exercise and then showed him my alternative plan for Europe. My fear was that I would be kicked out of his office and that this would be the end of my career. Something totally different happened. Patrick took his pen out and scribbled a couple of names on some paper. And he started to talk. He fully agreed with my conclusions and was endorsing the need for radical action. He wanted me to take a few weeks to discuss the new plan with a few outsiders, whom he trusted deeply. The most interesting name on the chart was Jimmy Allen from Bain & Company – Unilever had never worked with Bain before. I left the office really excited and ready to go to war.

The alternative plan

The simple plan that I had outlined on paper argued that we should:

- Reduce our cost of goods sold by several hundred basis points (bps), through a mixture of factory closures, better buying and improved efficiencies.
- Dramatically reduce our indirect costs/ overheads by 300–400 bps.
- Focus our activities on growing the core products and disposing of all non-core products and local jewels (see SepCo box on page 80).
- Increase the advertising spend behind our core brands.
- As a result of the above, bring our trading margins in line with the Unilever average, with a sustainable top line growth rate of 3–4%.

The harsh realities of the plan:

- Close some 25 factories.
- Reduce our European overheads by 30%, meaning that one in every three people would have to be made redundant. Including the disposal of assets, plants and entire businesses, the total workforce would be reduced from 55,000 to about 30,000 people.
- Accelerate the reorganization that had been announced in the previous months, such as outsourcing all of the transactional activities of finance and HR.
- Introduce one set of IT systems and processes for all European activities, create one supply chain company in Switzerland and reduce the number of operating companies from three in most countries to one in every country.

The beauty of the plan was the fact that it was holistic, complete and it addressed all the issues. The cost consequences were huge. Over €3 billion were needed to fund the restructuring. But, thanks to the cash generated from the disposals, the plan would be self-financing.

Because of the sensitivities, both internal and external, Patrick and I decided to keep it completely confidential and limit the number of people involved to a handful. Over the summer months, I was given access to the best brains in the strategy group. And I started to work with Jimmy Allen at Bain & Company. Jimmy and I clicked immediately, and soon after our first meeting, the first fresh ideas for the concept plan began to roll off the drawing board.

Gaining buy-in from my leadership team

In September, we organized a two-day meeting of my direct reports in Germany to discuss my conclusions. Of course, I had been talking to all of them individually and in small groups to discuss the key elements of the plan to reshape the portfolio, to reduce the costs and to revitalize the organization. I also reminded them of the conclusions of our week-long retreat at IMD. We reviewed the Unilever strategic planning process, and I told them about my sleepless night after the meeting of the Unilever Executive. I also told them about my early morning meeting with

Patrick and how I had got to know Jimmy Allen, whom I subsequently contracted to support me and then the European leadership team.

Jimmy took the team through his assessment of the current reality. It was quite a telling story, supported by the most shocking benchmark figures. The European team bought into the plan, with the exception of the local jewel recommendation. We decided to press on and spend more time on the future of the jewels in a subsequent meeting.

By December, the European team had reluctantly accepted the SepCo decision.

Aligning the Unilever Executive

My team prepared a full proposal for the restructuring project in record time. With a cost of over €3 billion, it was the biggest restructuring Europe had ever seen. When the proposal was presented to the Unilever Executive a few weeks later, it was a hard nut to swallow. The key issue was that there would be a lack of financial resources for the growth plans of my colleagues. However, Patrick and the CFO did a great job of convincing the members of the Executive and gaining their support for the proposal.

> ## insight
>
> *It is not clever to present a proposal in the middle of a leadershp changeover.*

SepCo: New home of the local jewels

The informal definition of a local jewel in Unilever is a successful brand that is sold in just one country. These brands often had a long lifespan, a good bond with the target audience in the country, above average profit margins and a strong growth rate. But unfortunately, this was not always the case. A number of so-called local jewels, mainly in northwestern Europe, did not fit this profile. In some cases, local management teams had a tendency to use or abuse these local jewels to optimize their results. For example, they would do this by milking the brands or buying volume to boost the overall growth picture of the country. The opposite was also sometimes the case. When the company as a whole was performing well above target, more money was channelled to the local jewels so they could advertise to get rid of the over delivery. The latter situation was very much to the joy of the local jewel brand team. Another issue for the local jewels was that the new organization with global brand teams and global/regional category management would mean that there would be no resources available to support these brands that were key contributors to the overheads of the local companies. Well-known examples of the local jewels included:
- BIFI and Peperami in Germany and the UK (ambient stable pocket sausages)
- Marmite in the UK.

Our solution was to remove responsibility for these brands from the local company boards and create a separate business unit in each country, which would be led by a dedicated person reporting to the head of SepCo (the name of the unit, which refers to "separate company"). In turn, the head of SepCo would report to me, the President of Unilever Europe. SepCo's head would not sit on my European leadership team and would have just one target to meet – cash! The objective of the local jewels was to generate cash, nothing else.

The head of the unit would have full freedom, as long as he/she was obeying the Unilever Code of Business and meeting the health, safety and quality standards.

It took a serious amount of hard negotiating and lobbying to gain the support of my Unilever Executive colleagues for this initiative. Thanks to the fact that Patrick liked the idea, we ultimately gained their support. Subsequently, it took months to get the local company chairmen on board. They of course realized that they were going to lose a large degree of freedom to manoeuvre their results. At a certain moment, I referred to it as, "The last battle in the war to end the totally independent local operating company." This was a major step towards a totally integrated European business that could grasp all the benefits of scale. In the end, I won all the fights with the exception of one. Germany convinced us that the Du Darfst brand (a slimming range) should not be considered a local jewel because it also had some margarine products in the range. I considered this exception a mistake on my side.

Executing on global priorities

James Allen
Partner
Bain & Company – www.bain.com

Like many other multinationals, Unilever was moving towards a more global model with local market leaders executing on global priorities. This required local managers to shift their attention away from single market brands to multi-market brands. The SepCo discussion in Schaffhausen had the potential to be a classic "win-lose" situation between the "region" and the "local markets".

In these situations, everyone in the room is faced with a series of management challenges:

1. **What hat do I wear?** The local managers must find the balance between representing their markets and being part of a regional and global leadership team. If they abdicate their local roles, the company could take decisions that go against local consumers and customers. On the other hand, if they only represent the local market, the company will only be as good as the sum of the local parts; it can't leverage global scale or set global priorities.

   In my view, the chairmen of the operating companies were outstanding leaders in the way they fought hard to show the unintended consequences of pursuing SepCo and as such, the final recommendations were adjusted for the better. In the end, they agreed with the decision because it made sense globally, even though it was not the best option for them locally.

   The lesson: Force teams to be clear on which "hat they are wearing" when approaching decisions. They must start local because only they can represent local consumers and customers. Then they must put on their regional or global hat.

2. **Do I tell or co-create?** Kees was faced with a real dilemma with SepCo. He needed to get two groups on board with the decision – the Unilever Executive team and Board and his own European Leadership Team (ELT). Because SepCo was part of a global strategy, he had to get CEO/Board approval first, which he did. Then he had to get his own ELT to agree to a decision the CEO had already made. Kees took a big risk that ultimately paid off – he fully trusted the leadership qualities of his team. He took the decision to the ELT and essentially said that even though the CEO had decided, he wouldn't pursue it without their agreement and support. He did this because "to tell" in this situation would have backfired. Kees mitigated the risk by forcing management to share the same fact base and journey of discovery he and the CEO had been on.

   The lesson: If you are going to "co-create" then bring the team fully into the tent – share the facts, the trade-offs and let them be part of the same journey you've been on. Trust them as leaders.

3. **When do I go bold?** Kees forced his team to think outside of the box on big changes that could be made. Deciding between incremental and bold change is one of the hardest leadership acts in business. The key test is: Which set of cost-reduction actions will allow my organization to most effectively refocus on growth and on serving our customers and consumers?

   The lesson: In every decision, make a choice between bold and incremental change. There is a solution for every situation. But what is wrong is to ignore either option.

BAIN & COMPANY

Getting board approval

The next hurdle was gaining the approval of the Unilever Board of Directors. Lots could go wrong with this, such as the proposal landing on the desk right in the middle of the handover of the Chairmanship from Antony Burgmans to Michael Treschow. This would not be a clever move, as we risked having the proposal rejected by the "old" board. So we decided to gradually prepare the board with a series of updates on Europe's performance, all the while hinting that we were studying more radical solutions. When we finally submitted the proposal, it sailed through the meeting. The best remark came from one of the board members asking me to begin the implementation "like tomorrow".

What a sleepless night can do!

The one-page handwritten radical plan addressing the European issues became a well thought through plan addressing all of the European Business Groups' issues and problems. It was supported by the full executive team, the Unilever Executive and the Board. It met most of its targets and luckily prepared the European business for the economic crisis that followed. My sleepless night had paid off!

Tom's Column

Unleashing the power of employees – the true impact of leadership

Thomas Malnight
IMD Professor
www.imd.org

In many organizations, leaders outsource the challenge of thinking about the future of their organizations to consultants. Instead, they focus on the mundane management of day-to-day operations. This has led to complacency and compliance increasingly becoming the norm for many organizations. It has also resulted in individuals focusing only on managing their silos.

Leaders often talk about empowerment and engagement, but the way they lead their businesses often results in the opposite. From my 20-plus years of experience as an academic working with countless leadership teams around the world, Kees has been one of the best exceptions to this situation. Leaders struggle with challenges, personal and professional, but they also have a direct impact on the lives of thousands of other individuals, and their families, every day. In all of the stories that you read in this book, I suggest you take a close look at the impact each situation and event has on the other individuals involved. The power of successful leaders is in the impact they have on their organizations and the lives they touch through their actions.

Imagine, if you can, a team of successful senior executives who want to change their organization in an unprecedented way and their leader who after a "sleepless night" takes on the responsibility of finally addressing the real challenges. Imagine, if you can, a group of leaders who are used to preparing yet another set of documents that everyone knows will not be practiced, but then they are confronted in a "tent" by someone saying that they will be held accountable for all documents and plans they sign. Imagine, if you can, being part of a group of 1,500 individuals who have been brought together to talk about how they must change their behaviors, from top to bottom, to move the organization forward. Imagine, if you can, a leader who tells you to take time out with your colleagues to show how the company has "Hearts for Kids" in each of the communities in which it operates.

For me, this book is as much about personal insights and lessons as it is about professional impact. It is about a leader who provides the space and opportunity to work in a different way, a leader who truly engages and empowers the individuals in his organization, and a leader who cares about the impact he has on the organization and the world around him.

REFLECTIONS

In this chapter, I have shared with you five very different stories. However, they have one common message. It is essential for leaders to find the right vehicle to get a key message communicated to the people in their organization – and communicated in such a way that the people understand the message, understand the need for change and feel part of the solution because they have been engaged in the creation of the way forward. They "own" the solution and feel committed to the success of the organization.

Team alignment, team commitment to each other's success and team spirit need to be created, cultivated, nurtured and protected. There is nothing more important in achieving your objectives than a winning team. To get there, the leader has to lead with courage. The leader has to be willing to move beyond the comfort zone, confront issues and take difficult decisions, having listened to different inputs from team members. A leader must agree with his or her team, that he or she is empowered and trusted to take the necessary decisions.

You will have noticed that I have used very different types of events to get my messages across, sometimes involving just my direct reports, sometimes my entire management group, whatever was appropriate for the situation.

You will also have noticed that I have used very different leadership approaches – ranging from autocratic to participative – for the different situations in which I found myself. Some styles will feel more comfortable than others will, but your feelings in this respect are not important; you have to do what is required in the specific situation.

Notes

[1] This section has been adapted from Killing, Peter, Thomas Malnight with Tracey Keys. Must-Win Battles: *How to win them, again and again.* Harlow, UK: Pearson International Learning, 2005.

[2] All of whom were involved in the discussion.

[3] Killing, Peter, Thomas Malnight with Tracey Keys. *Must-Win Battles: How to win them, again and again.* Harlow, UK: Pearson International Learning, 2005.

[4] Killing, Peter, Thomas Malnight and Tracey Keys. Jan Ryan, CEO (A). IMD case no. IMD-3-1574, 2005.
Killing, Peter, Thomas Malnight and Tracey Keys. Jan Ryan, CEO (B): Going Home. IMD case no. IMD-3-1575, 2005.

[5] An elevator speech is a short overview that can be delivered in the same amount of time as an elevator ride – about 30 seconds.

Understanding the power of self-regeneration

4

Reaching a level of total balance requires more than just dividing your time among the many roles you play in your professional and personal lives – business leader, father, husband, friend – and your role in society. You must also stay fit – physically, emotionally and spiritually. It is only when your spirit, mind and body are perfectly aligned that you can claim that you have reached a level of "total balance". In this chapter, I will share three stories about how I discovered the importance of looking after yourself.

insight

Reaching a level of total balance requires more than just dividing your time among the many roles you play in your professional and personal lives … you must also stay fit – physically, emotionally and spiritually.

MONTANA: A MOMENT OF DEEP SELF-REFLECTION

It was July 2005 when I left Yellowstone National Park behind me. I was deeply impressed by its natural beauty, the overwhelming effects of the Rocky Mountains and the endless forests filled with wildlife. My instructions said that I had to leave the main road, turn onto a dirt road and follow it for 52 miles. As I drove along, I felt I had all the time in the world

... in this chapter

- **Montana**
- **Taking control**
- **Getting in touch with your inner self**
- **Reflections**

Montana: Endless fields of cows

insight

If you want to take control and stay in control of your life, a vision quest is the best way to clarify your purpose and your top five priorities.

to reflect on why I was here and what I wanted to experience. The mountains were becoming friendlier, agricultural land started to appear, and along with it lots of cows, but hardly any people. Montana is a vast, sprawling state of wide prairies, dense forests, majestic mountains, mighty rivers and a sparse population.

During one of my stops at yet another beautiful spot to enjoy the splendorous nature, I thought of Joseph Jaworski who started me on this journey. As director of Unilever's Foods Division, I became involved in the Partnership for Child Nutrition. Unilever, together with Synergos and Generon (Joseph's company), formed this initiative to develop sustainable solutions for the millions of children in India who were dying from starvation. As Unilever was in the food business and was the largest company in India, we could help make a difference by applying our capabilities in terms of nutrition, marketing and distribution, not to mention the influence we could apply on the local authorities.

During one of Joseph's visits to my Rotterdam office, he argued at length that we should take the Partnership for

Child Nutrition team through the famous U-process,[1] (which he developed with others and which I will explain in more detail later). I did not understand the process fully, but I was intrigued with one aspect – becoming one with nature by spending three days alone in the mountains. I happen to love nature, and I have never had three days on my own, so I found the combination captivating. To make a long story short, Joseph got me an invitation to attend the vision quest, which he and a special branch of McKinsey were organizing for Synergos and its Global Philanthropists Circle (GPC), which was founded by Peggy Dulany (Synergos'

Chair) and her father David Rockefeller. I loved the idea of getting to know Peggy because I had heard so many great things about her and the fantastic work she was doing in bringing together the leading philanthropic families from around the world who were committed to using their time, influence and resources to fight global poverty and social injustice. In short, there were many reasons why I wanted to participate in this 10-day quest.

As I continued along the dirt road, all signs of civilization were left well behind me. I noticed that my cell phone had lost its connection; hence, my connection with the modern world was gone. I was happy that I

Peggy's ranch in Montana

insight

Discover your destiny and live it out wholly and resolutely.

had topped up my fuel tank before leaving the main road. For a moment, I wondered what I would do if the car broke down. My conclusion – just sit and wait.

When I finally arrived at Peggy's ranch, I was greeted with a very warm welcome. One by one the other participants along with eight organizers and support staff arrived – some 25 in total. Included in the group were philanthropists from South Africa, Brazil, Columbia, the US, France, the UK and Ireland, quite a number of females, organizers from the US and Australia, and two "strange" Dutch businessmen from Unilever.

Getting started

The formal introductions were short. We sat in a large circle in a converted barn. Joseph asked the first question: "What did you learn from your mother and father that helps explain why you are here?" This question broke the ice. Very meaningful and emotional stories emerged, which enabled us to connect immediately. Subsequently, we went into the deeper purpose of the event, which was described as "discovering your own destiny, living it out wholly and resolutely". This was based on four insights on the theory of destiny:

- There is a basic human need to discover your purpose and to serve this purpose.
- If you look for signs, you will find them in the most unexpected places.
- The universe provides helping hands, but it requires deep intention and risk-it-all commitment and conviction.
- You will lose the stumbling blocks and antidotes you encounter along the way.

As I listened to the stories and the explanations about the purpose of the next 10 days, I had mixed feelings. My original purpose was to disappear into nature for a few days by myself, not to listen to all these "soft" philosophical conversations. But I was also beginning to understand the deeper meaning behind the words "purpose" and "destiny".

The Invitation

(Excerpt) By Oriah[2]

It doesn't interest me
what you do for a living.
I want to know
what you ache for
and if you dare to dream
of meeting your heart's longing.

It doesn't interest me
how old you are.
I want to know
if you will risk
looking like a fool
for love
for your dream
for the adventure of being alive.

It doesn't interest me
what planets are
squaring your moon ...
I want to know
if you have touched
the centre of your own sorrow
if you have been opened

by life's betrayals
or have become shrivelled and closed
from fear of further pain.

I want to know
if you can sit with pain
mine or your own
without moving to hide it
or fade it
or fix it.

I want to know
if you can be with joy
mine or your own
if you can dance with wildness
and let the ecstasy fill you
to the tips of your fingers and toes without
cautioning us
to be careful
to be realistic
to remember the limitations
of being human and therefore trustworthy.

Printed with permission of the author.

For the next three days, every session began with a few lines from the *Book of Readings*.[3] Initially, I could not concentrate on listening to them. But gradually they started to capture my attention and some of them really struck a chord. "The Invitation", a poem by the Oriah Mountain Dreamer, has since come to mean a lot to me.

In the days that followed, we learnt a lot by talking, sharing and developing a better understanding of what was going to happen to us when we spent three full days – 72 hours – on our own in the mountains.

Getting prepared

Before heading out, we had to understand some of the theory behind the U-process. The objective is to get from reacting to regenerating and the U-process helps us understand what regenerating means and how to get there. In order to create the proper environment for regeneration, the U-process takes us through three phases – sensing, presencing and realizing.[4]

When I look back on all the elements of the preparation, I fully understand why it was so important. Only when you are able to get your brain frequency down to the lowest possible level, will you be able to access your creativity and intuition. High altitudes, meditation and fasting all contribute significantly towards lowering your brain frequency.

Another element of the preparation that had an impact on me was the fact that we were on Indian holy land and that

The U-Process[5]

I. Sensing
Observe Current Reality

III. Realizing
Enact New Reality

II. Presencing
Retreat and Reflect

During the first phase – sensing – you uncover an accurate picture of your current reality. In order to do this, you must develop two capacities – suspending judgment and redirecting. Suspending judgment means being aware of your own personal biases and mental maps and how and when they are affecting your perceptions. Redirecting is the ability to listen and see things from different perspectives rather than from within yourself. In the second phase – presencing – you retreat and reflect to deepen your understanding of the role you are playing in your current reality. There are two capacities that must be developed during this phase – letting go and letting come. Letting go means putting yourself into a state of profound openness. Letting come is when new ideas and a new understanding of your vocation is born. Spending time alone in nature helps you to understand with profound clarity what your course of action must be.

The third phase – realizing – is the crystallizing phase when new realities are enacted – when you implement your course of action.

We also learnt to meditate and in the mornings we were taught Tai Chi. It was also explained to us why the entire process would benefit from fasting. We also studied how the brain works, which is how I discovered that one can distinguish four groups of brain frequencies:

- Beta is the highest frequency, with 14–38 cycles per second (cps). Here you are thinking rationally and logically.
- Alpha is often referred to as the state of one-pointed focus (8–14 cps).
- Theta is the state in which you can become creative and find solutions to problems (4–8 cps).
- Delta is the state in which you can access your intuition (0.5–4 cps).

we should have some understanding of
their religion and rituals and respect for
the Indian culture. We learnt the meaning
behind the four wind directions, which I
recalled later when I had a very memorable
encounter with the west wind.

- In the North, you will find your purpose.
  It is the area of wisdom, and it is
  symbolized by the wolf.
- The East, where the sun rises, is of
  course the zone of birth and luminosity,
  and it is symbolized by the eagle.
- In the South, you will find love, open
  heartedness and courage, symbolized
  by the deer.
- The West is the area of not only death
  but also rebirth, and it is symbolized by
  the mythical thunderbird.

We also got some very interesting insights
into the cosmos. The sky in Montana – also
known as Big Sky Country – is very clear
because of the lack of pollution. You see
stars and planets that you have never seen
before, some of which are light years away.
It makes you realize just how tiny you are in
the universe.

Finally, the importance of "shared
intentions" – a shared objective developed
by deep listening in a safe environment –
became very clear. You cannot make

a mistake; every contribution is a great
contribution. It is safe to speak out. Joseph
often talked about the fact that "the genius
is in the collectiveness". I have discovered
some great evidence that this is often
the power of great teams. And more
importantly, it is a way to build great teams.

On the move: The presencing phase

We were taken by jeep to a totally
secluded base camp at the foot of a high
mountain. It was the middle of summer
and temperatures were soaring down
in the valley, but they asked us to bring
really warm clothes, so I had gloves,
thermal underwear, a hat and a mountain
jacket with me. We also had to bring bear
spray, a mosquito net and repellent, an
emergency walkie-talkie, a flashlight and
sufficient batteries. Anything else we
needed would be by each of our tents.
Watches, smartphones, pens, paper,
books and games were all supposed to
be left behind. They did not check our
backpacks, but most of us followed their
instructions. I did as well, except for a tiny
notebook and a pen.

At one point we performed a ritual that
signified the end of our talking and the
beginning of our fasting. As we walked in
total silence, our nerves were heightened
and our hearts began to beat faster. I do
not know what was happening with our
brain frequencies, but there was definitely
a mixture of excitement and fear racing
through our bodies and minds.

In deep silence, we walked up the
mountain in groups of six behind one of the
guides. Despite the altitude, there were
still lots of trees. The path was narrow,
windy and at times steep. The views were
gorgeous. Every so many kilometres, we
would reach a campsite, where one of us
would be left with his or her tent. It was
always a surprise when a tent suddenly
appeared out of nowhere in a beautifully
sheltered place. Every spot had its own
unique characteristics, and each one was
even more beautiful than the last one. My
turn did not come until the end. I was the
last one to be dropped off, so five times
I hugged and silently wished each of my
new friends courage, fun and wisdom.
Of course, since we were not allowed to
talk, this was all communicated using body
language. And each time, one of my friends
was dropped off I was envious because
every spot was absolutely extraordinary and
full of elements I loved. But on we went
for another 10 or 15 minutes ending in my
vision of a dream world.

My tent was situated under the few
remaining trees on the edge of the
mountain overlooking the Rockies. The
view was unobstructed for as far as the
human eye could see. There was nothing
between me and infinity. There was still
a small patch of snow on the ground
and a little stream of crystal clear water
was floating down the mountain some
50 meters from my tent. The grass was
about 20 centimetres high and filled with

wildflowers. I loved it. And I couldn't help wondering why I was the lucky one to get the best spot on the mountain. This was my home – my nirvana – for the next 72 hours. I was ecstatic.

Making camp

For the first little while on a discovery tour, if you are action-driven like me, you feel you have to do something. So, I went into the tent, which was a tiny, thin shelter just big enough to fit me. I unpacked the bag in the tent and discovered a good quality sleeping bag, but no mattress. Then, I quickly dug a toilet in a place where the branches of a fallen tree provided a seat. Next, I made a

Nothing between me and infinity

sundial. I knew more or less what time it was and I knew the times of sunset and sunrise and that the sun is at its highest point at 12 noon. This allowed me to interpolate the rest of the points on the clock.

We got clear instructions not to go more than 100 steps away from our tent. So, I took several sticks of wood and placed them 100 steps away from my tent in every direction. I cheated a little, as I wanted the patch of snow to be part of my land. Next, I walked through the high grass from stick to stick. The result was a beautiful circle laying out my territory. And then – nothing – there was nothing else to do. So, here I was, on my own, on top of a mountain some 3,500 meters high, with beautiful sunshine, no wind and hardly any sounds – just peace and lots of time to reflect.

But, there was one more thing I could do. I scattered a lot of dead wood around my tent so that I could hear if animals approached during the night – as if you really want to know if a bear is sniffing around your tent. Also, there was a bear bag that was hanging from a high branch on a tree that contained a few granola bars, some dried fruit and a few lemons and some spice that I was to use to make a special drink that I would sip every 10 minutes to take my hunger away. Making the special drink was really the last thing on my invisible to-do list. I mixed some lemon juice and cayenne pepper with water, shook it and took a small sip.

And then I sat on my rock, stared into the endless, limitless world and started to think.

Dealing with an overdose of time

I thought about all the things that had happened over the last three days. I thought about all my new friends, and I wondered what they were doing. I could even picture a few of them sitting in front of their tents. I began to wonder why I had tears in my eyes while I was listening to some of the stories we had shared during the previous three days. And, then, all of a sudden, I became completely overwhelmed by the beauty of my little home on top of the mountain.

I started to meditate. I found that every time I meditated I was learning, getting better and I was able to go deeper. In the beginning, the flies were hindering me, but I was soon able to put them out of my mind. I had conversations with "the South". I went for long walks along my circular border path. I played with the water in my little stream. I did my Tai Chi movements. I laughed, I shouted, I cried, I stared into space. And, I started to think about my life, my deeper purpose, my lovely wife Renée, my great kids, my current role in Unilever, my friends, my mother, my father who had died 25 years ago, my other family members. I started to explore the quality of my relationships. I concluded that I had to bring more romance into the relationship between Renée and myself. I realized that I had to be much nicer and more patient with my mother. I found that my life was out of balance. Unilever was absorbing too much time, and not enough time was left over for the boys or the FSHD Foundation. I came to the firm conclusion that this had to change.

On another level, I concluded that the Unilever of 2005 was no longer my Unilever. It had changed a lot and had moved from being an absolutely unique company with family values to being just another one among the hordes of other companies. In my opinion, it had lost its heart and soul – not a great conclusion to reach sitting alone on a rock 3,500 meters above sea level. I decided to address this issue with my bosses, the two Chairmen, and my Unilever Executive colleagues when I returned from Montana.

Mother Earth has a message

After a good night's sleep in my tiny shelter, I woke up early. The weather did not look too good. Threatening clouds were starting to appear on the horizon. After eating a few nuts and drinking lots of water, I started my rituals, first, by walking around my path several times, thinking about nothing. As I

Joseph's Column

Nature as a portal to renewal and transformation

Joseph Jaworski
Chairman
Generon International – www.generoninternational.com

The story Kees told of his Montana retreat provides a precise picture of the power of nature as a portal to renewal and transformation. Kees spoke of the "profound effect" the retreat had on him. The "amazing insights" that came to him changed him and led him to "make important decisions" in his life. In his closing remarks, Kees suggested that if a management team participated in such a retreat, it could become "unbeatable" and able to "perform wonders". The views that Kees has expressed are, in my opinion, not overstatements.

I have been privileged to lead such wilderness retreats now for over three decades; without exception, I see these same results year after year. Why is this so? The wilderness passage provides a liminal experience, the root from which our highest features and experiences can grow – where self-realization is born and over time, it matures into a distinctive kind of awareness that has been described in the ancient texts for thousands of years. It is found among the traditional beliefs of people in every region of the world, and in its fully developed form, it has its place among every one of the world's higher religions. Such a passage for a management team acts to dissolve the team's self-imposed boundaries enabling it to operate as a single intelligence for the good of its institution and society.

Generon International

started trying to listen to my body, I noticed all kinds of different reactions. The strange thing was that I got the same feelings in my body on the same parts of the path during each round. Then I began to wonder if this was a coincidence, or if it was determined by the powers of the four winds. Or, did my awareness about this phenomenon become a self-fulfilling prophecy? I would ask Joseph when I returned to the base camp. Just as I was mulling over these important questions, raindrops started to fall from the sky. I could not believe my eyes when the raindrops froze the moment they touched my body. This was a typical example of undercooled rain, which I remembered learning about in my school days. I stood there for a while, with my arms spread wide, letting the drops form ice on my arms and shoulders. The rain soon turned into hail though, and thunder and lightning were fast approaching. Actually, the thunderstorms were coming from three directions, and they looked as if they were going to collide right above me. The hailstones were now the size of large marbles, and they were starting to hurt me. It was time to disappear into my tent. Then all hell broke loose. The temperature dropped dramatically, and I became bitterly cold. I put on all my sweaters, a pair of gloves and a woollen hat. Then, I got into my sleeping bag, but I was still pretty cold.

The Thunderbird

After a while, I fell into a deep sleep. When I woke up, the thunderstorms had vanished, and it was very quiet outside.

I had to get out of my tent for two good reasons; I wanted to get a feeling for the time and I needed a relief break. The atmosphere outside was special. There were a few huge clouds hanging against a deep blue sky. The cloud in the west was a strange shape, and the sun was shining behind it. Throughout the early evening, I could not stop looking at this particular cloud over and over again. I began to wonder what it was about it that was attracting me and intriguing me. Then, all of a sudden, I knew. The cloud was in the shape of the thunderbird. Nobody had ever

seen this creature, but here it was staring at me with one eye (which was formed by a little hole in the cloud). What did this mean? Was there a message? Was this a signal that I had been reborn? I found this an interesting thought.

And with that thought, I went back to bed. In the middle of the night, a sort of tremble or shock woke me up. Then, I heard a lot of barking from the shepherd's dogs down in the valley. I was not bothered at all. In my half-awake state, I guessed that a moose had found a nice place to sleep, close to my tent. I found this a reassuring thought.

Later, I learnt that the shock was actually a small earthquake – 4.5 on the Richter scale – with the epicentre about 50 km away from us. I also heard that the wind that came with the thunderstorms had been so severe that it had knocked trees down. In fact, one tree fell right above the tent in which Precious, a beautiful young woman from South Africa, was sleeping. It was a miracle that another tree broke its fall just one metre above her tent. The emergency team was called in, and they moved her tent to another position. Several of the others had also used their walkie-talkies to find out what had happened, or to ask for extra blankets to stay warm in the cold.

Using pen and pencil

The next day was quite different. The sun was shining, there was no wind and hardly any clouds. It was about time to wash myself in my little snow patch. After my morning rituals, I began writing in my tiny notebook. For hours, I poured out all of my thoughts onto the paper, and along the way, I added a few tears. It felt great to be able to share my feelings and emotions with that tiny piece of paper. Even now – almost five years later – similar emotions surface when I reread my notes.

One of the stupid things I remember doing was stepping out of my 100-metre circle each day. I did this simply to prove to myself that nobody could limit my movements. If I wanted to cross the line, I would. It gave me a great sense of freedom. And when I jumped back into my boundaries, I was filled with enthusiasm because I had dared to take this step.

Back to reality

All of a sudden, a horse and one of the guides appeared behind me. I had been completely ensconced in a higher sphere, so I didn't hear or see him coming. It was time to pack up and walk back down to the base camp. One by one, we met the others at their campsites, all of whom were very much affected by seeing familiar faces again. Back at the base camp, we broke our silence and attacked a special meal. Everything tasted great; it was a delight to enjoy all the different tastes and flavours.

Seated in a circle on the grass, we had our first session to share our facts from the last three days. We told each other

My notebook still stirs my emotions

what had really happened, how we lived, how we killed time, how we coped with the weather. In the evening, we had another session, this time about our emotions, our dreams and our feelings. Beautiful stories emerged. Amazing insights – some very personal – came out. We all jumped in to support each other during this process to help each other deal with these new insights. In the lodges, where we were housed in small groups of four, the sharing continued. In my group's case, we were seated in the jacuzzi under the stars, drinking a fantastic glass of wine.

The last day was about preparing for the return trip home – how to deal with your partner, your friends, your

colleagues and your relatives. They had not experienced what we had, so nothing had changed for them. They would not have the slightest idea what we had been through, so the reunion had to be handled with care.

We also had to make some real commitments to address the issues that we had determined needed to be addressed. This was to ensure that we would hold ourselves accountable for the promises we made to ourselves.

My commitment

My key take-away from the group was that I seemed to have a unique set of individual strengths. If joined together, these strengths could give me the power to re-establish the balance among the important things in my life – my family, Unilever, and my muscular dystrophy activities for broader society.

I would also buy the DVD "Shall We Dance", with Richard Gere and Jennifer Lopez in the lead roles, at the airport and watch it with my wife Renée. This was my symbolic way of saying, "I love you and I know all too well what you have missed and miss."

Leaving Montana behind

When the time came to leave, it felt like we were leaving our closest friends behind. There are very few people in the world that I have shared as many emotions with as I did with this group. Before leaving, we sang a final song.

The final song

We will all go together
To our pure crystal fountain
And around it we shall place
All the flowers of the mountain

Let us go friends go
And we will all strive together
To create a better world
Full of love and compassion

Let us go friends ... go.

Back in the office

After talking a lot about my experience at home, it was quite special to return to the office and find that the team was interested in hearing about my experience. At that point, I realized how fortunate I had been to attend such a unique retreat. I felt privileged.

The Chairman reacted without emotion to my revelation that, in my eyes, Unilever was losing its heart and soul. He was more interested in the personal experience. It was great to learn that a year later he also went on the retreat. My story had clearly had an impact on him.

Patrick, the CEO, wanted a better understanding of how I had arrived at my conclusion about Unilever. He immediately started to brainstorm ways we could address the issue. He was very interested in hearing what I was going to do to get a better balance among work, family and the FSHD.

A year later, after a couple of good months of keeping things in balance, I noticed that I was falling back into my old pattern of working 80 to 100 hours per week. My time was being consumed by my top priority at Unilever – securing the European business and bringing it back to a position of sustainable growth.

I have shared my Montana experience with you because it had a profound effect on me. It changed me. It made me more well-rounded and, ultimately, it led to an important decision. My recommendation to every leader is to build time into your calendar – at least a full day away from the office and preferably in nature – for personal reflection.

insight

Every leader should build time into his or her calendar – at least a full day away from the office and preferably in nature – for personal reflection.

Peggy's Column

The value of disconnecting from daily life

Peggy Dulany
Founder & Chair
The Synergos Institute – www.synergos.org

Kees's description of the "deep dive" he took while on retreat in the wilderness demonstrates the value of disconnecting from daily life to assess one's life and prepare for change – or recommitment.

Why is it that spending time in the wilderness is so powerful in this regard? In my view – and that of many wilderness guides with whom I have worked – we are held by Mother Earth at the same time as we are stripped bare of all pretence, of our mask, by the challenges of being alone with our fears, which often appear to be "out there", but are revealed to be "in here". Confronting those fears and honing ourselves back to the essence of our soul's purpose in this life is intensely clarifying.

This takes courage and is best done with competent guides in a group setting, being adequately prepared ahead of time for the solo experience and helped to integrate the learning into life going forward.

Fasting helps speed up the "dropping down" process in which one enters almost a dream state from which it is possible to access insights and feelings from the unconscious that

our action-oriented work minds may obscure from us. Feeling the freedom to imagine a thunderbird in a cloud, to test our boundaries, to cry our heart out, not even knowing why, to have conversations with animals or trees, releases our creative imagination to see things differently and to solve problems that previously seemed unsolvable.

Then returning to the group, with whom one has developed deep trust, and telling the story validates the learning. Committing to next steps in front of the group adds gravity to the decisions taken. But most of all, in the return to the every day, the images of the wild, the storms, the magical beauty of the mountains, the view from our campsite, persist and inspire and remind us of our discoveries and commitments every time we are tempted to return to life as it once was.

TAKING CONTROL: MY EARLY RETIREMENT DECISION

The first quarter of the year is the time that the appraisal discussions take place everywhere in the organization. In March 2007, Patrick Cescau and I also had a meeting to discuss my 2006 performance. I was well prepared for two reasons. First, the members of the Unilever Executive were all asked to participate in an extensive 360-degree feedback exercise. About 12 people participated in every appraisal. In my case, the group of participants consisted of five colleagues from the Executive, Patrick and six members from my team. Second, I was not really happy with my job and the support I was getting for the European restructuring ideas.

I was pleased with the outcome of the feedback. Interestingly, there was a difference in the perceptions of the two groups – my colleagues on the Executive and my team members. The Executive felt that I was siding with my European business group too much and my team members felt that I was defending the interests of Unilever in general too much. I concluded from this that I probably had struck the right balance between the two roles that I was playing – leading Europe and being a member of Unilever's top team.

In August 2006, I had my sleepless night (Chapter 4), during which I concluded that the strategy for Unilever Europe needed a fundamental rethink. In the subsequent months, we designed a plan that would bring the European business back to growth, while dramatically reducing the total costs of the operation. We got the approval in principle, but nothing happened. Unilever was at a crossroads. It had decided to move towards a non-executive Chairman of the Board, rather than an executive Chairman. This meant a number of changes on the board. It was considered better to wait until these changes were announced to submit the plan to reshape the European business. This would give the new Chairman the chance to consider the plans, which would require billions of restructuring funds. This was a plausible argument, but also frustrating because we were potentially forgoing some significant savings during the months of waiting. It was also very difficult to explain to the team who had worked day and night to build a solid plan. As a leader, I had to balance the interests of Unilever and the European business. In the end, we accepted the delay in the final decision-making process as we could not risk rejection.

All of this did not make me a very happy person. The tensions were high. I had to spend an enormous amount of time, first in the design phase and then in the development of the detailed plans and lobbying of all kinds of stakeholders –

from my own team all the way to the European Union Commissioners. In the meantime, we had to deliver our targets under these circumstances. I found myself working 80 to 100 hours per week dealing with the magnitude of issues, which clearly left no time for the FSHD Foundation, family, friends or hobbies. I felt a moral obligation to continue to challenge the numbers of the plan, particularly the total number of jobs that would have to disappear. About a third of the approximately 55,000 employees would lose their jobs or would go with their part of the business to a new owner. I wanted to be absolutely sure that there was no alternative for every job that would be lost. I wanted to be able to look myself in the mirror and answer the question: Did I evaluate every possible alternative? This was clearly the hardest part.

Against this backdrop, we had our discussion about my performance.

Looking ahead

At my 2007 performance meeting, Patrick and I decided not to look back; instead, we discussed the remarks made by the assessors in the 360-degree appraisal. We talked about how to create space in my calendar. And we reflected on the outcome of the Montana retreat. I recalled that some years ago Patrick had suggested a practical way to deal with an overloaded agenda. He had told me to write my top five priorities down on a piece of paper and then remove everything – yes EVERYTHING – from my agenda that was not directly related to my priorities. It is a painful exercise, but it is amazing how much "rubbish" finds its way into your calendar, and how much space you can create in your daily life by going through this exercise. Despite having gone through the exercise again, my calendar was once more becoming overloaded. Of course, I was the one who allowed this situation to emerge because I say "yes" too easily to requests for meetings, interviews, counselling sessions and representative activities. That is one of my biggest weaknesses! I was falling back into the same trap over and over again. It was time to consider a different solution.

Patrick and I reached the conclusion that it might be worthwhile for me to consider an early retirement from Unilever. Several aspects needed to be evaluated before reaching a final decision. We had to look into the contractual arrangements, the net income implications, the pension rights, the timing and the communication process. In order to keep things under control we would only involve the head of HR, Sandy Ogg.

A few weeks later, we concluded that it was possible and affordable for me to take an early retirement. We agreed that I would see the future Chairman of Unilever to explain my situation and to seek his agreement. We also concluded that it would be extremely important for the credibility of the European restructuring plan that the announcement of my retirement would not be made before the end of March 2008 – almost a year away. This was not a problem for me. By agreeing to an early retirement in principle, I could see the end in sight and this created some peace of mind for me. It also meant that I would be able to start implementing the restructuring plan – of which I had been the architect – and then take the first hit after the restructuring announcements, deal with the reactions and smooth the way for my successor to finish the job (still a mammoth task).

It was important to embark on an orderly process with regard to the announcement of and departure date for my retirement. We agreed upon the Annual General Meeting (AGM) in May 2008 as my departure date, and this would be announced when the AGM agenda and papers were distributed in March 2008. We also agreed not to tell anybody, except of course the members of the Remuneration and Nominations Committee of the Board. It is always very difficult to keep secrets in Unilever, but this time we managed.

I focused on the implementation of the plan to rejuvenate the European business. The big announcement of the restructuring in Europe followed in the second half of 2007. About half of the plan had been implemented by the time I left.

Interestingly, in hindsight, some of my team members said they noticed a remarkable difference in my mood and temper during my last year. I was more determined than ever but less stressed because I had become much more balanced. The decision had clearly created a feeling of relief in my mind, which had a positive impact on my effectiveness as a leader.

The announcement

The days before the announcement were pretty hectic. I wanted to inform as many colleagues, family, friends and relations as possible by phone. Of course, this was not possible. There was only a small window of time between 9 o'clock the previous night and 8 o'clock the following morning, just before the Amsterdam stock exchange opened. Therefore, I decided to call family and direct reports, and write to all other stakeholders. A big advantage of today's electronic world is that you can prepare everything, upload it and with the press of a button, the messages are sent at the precise time. After it went public, I spend the rest of the day, responding to a series of beautiful and heart-warming reactions.

There was some press interest. *Het Financieele Dagblad* [6] wanted an interview and a few photos. We had all been trained to deal with the press, and we had been warned of all the risks. I agreed to be interviewed. For whatever reason the interviewer and I connected well. He liked my story to the extent that he wanted to make it the lead article in the personal

I lost sight of my priorities

section of the Saturday supplement. The rest of the week, he asked me many more clarifying questions. The resulting article was a really good reflection of the true story.

The Power of Balance Symposium

It was very rewarding to see the amount of attention, care and dedication that had gone into organizing several farewell events. I had one dream that Patrick was kind enough to help me realize. I wanted to organize a special symposium for colleagues, friends, family and relations

at the Unilever Research Laboratories in Vlaardingen. It was the ideal place to hold such an event, and it was my intention to bring together a unique gathering of speakers around the theme of the "Power of Balance". This was the first time that I started to use these words in public. In my welcome speech, I explained my concept of total balance. Then I handed the microphone over to the presenters. All had been part of my Unilever and FSHD journey over the last 10 to 15 years.

Jan Reker, the general manager of PSV Eindhoven (the primary football league in the Netherlands) explained why he had created Spieren voor Spieren. He also spoke about how to create a team out of a number of individual talented football players. Annie McKee from the Teleos Leadership Institute described what it takes to become a resonant leader and did this in a very personal and warm way. Professor Theo Verrips, the science specialist for the FSHD Foundation, explained the FSHD's research programme. Professor Tom Malnight from IMD spoke about the importance of a long-term perspective in driving a company forward. Patrick Cescau closed the session with a very powerful call for more CSR and other responsible actions on the part of corporations, such as taking responsibility for an organization's impact on the environment. Then, on behalf of Unilever, he handed over a large cheque to the treasurer of the FSHD Foundation.

We also used the opportunity to encourage participation in the large bicycle event, The Amstel Gold Race, in April 2009. We wanted to get a team of at least 100 cyclists to participate on the FSHD team to raise money for the Foundation. The group of young Unilever managers who had organized this two years earlier for Hearts for Kids (see Chapter 2), offered me, as a farewell present, the opportunity to organize this fundraising event. Arguably, this was one of the most beautiful presents I could receive. The hearts of these young managers were clearly touched by the support they received for their event

The Power of Balance presenters: Annie McKee, Tom Malnight, Jan Reker

through my participation in the 125 km cycle race. Our encouragement worked so well that 350(!) people signed up to participate and sign their friends and family up as sponsors. It was a fantastic success with over €110,000 raised for the Foundation. And most importantly, it has become a tradition. We continue to participate every year in this famous cycle event.

I could not have imagined a more rewarding way to start my new life as "a pensionado", with fundraising for FSHD research as my top priority.

GETTING IN TOUCH WITH YOUR INNER SELF: THE POWER OF AUTHENTICITY

In my last years as Unilever's President of Europe, we started to pay more and more attention to 360-degree feedback. We found it to be a very useful tool for the Unilever Executive and Board to gain good insights into people for succession planning purposes.

I took this part of my job very seriously, so I spent a lot of time reading and analyzing the 360-degree assessments of my people. One of the things that struck me was that several of the assessments mentioned a lack of genuineness or authenticity in some of my direct reports. Targets had been met and the scores on the key metrics were good. A lot of hard work had gone into addressing the improvement suggestions from the previous year. In general, good progress had been made, but there was still something missing. Authenticity was becoming the topic of more and more of my appraisal conversations with my team members. So I started to coach them on being more authentic. But I was struggling with describing what I meant by authenticity. Acting and staying genuine, exposing yourself, giving more of yourself all came to mind.

In the late 1990s, I had worked a lot with Tom Gross and Arri Pauw of Genesis. This was a small consultancy firm that had been recruited by Roy Brown, the President of Unilever Foods Europe, to help us design a new operating framework for our business group. Together with the key members of Roy's team, they developed the so-called 4-cornerstone model, which divided our complex organization into four pillars: Roy's leadership team, the product categories, the functions and the countries. To gain acceptance for the new framework, which bears a striking resemblance to Unilever's operating framework today, we organized a number of large management gatherings. As Roy's right hand, I worked very closely with Arri and Tom and had great respect for both of them.

After retiring from Unilever, I met up with Arri to compare my leadership studies at IMD with their work. Arri told me about a weeklong session that he runs several times a year for six to nine business leaders in Frandeux, a lovely town in the Ardennes in Belgium. Even though I was retired, we quickly reached the conclusion that by attending, I could gain some real insights into the meaning of "authenticity" that I could pass along in my role as an Executive-in-Residence at IMD.

Frandeux

The objective of the Frandeux session was to unleash the participants' full potential to deal with delivering results through developing their awareness of and mastery over their emotions and subsequent behaviour. In April 2009, I had the privilege of attending one of these sessions now described in Arri's great book – *The Road Within: In Search of Authentic Leadership Behavior.*[8] The programme had four parts: 1) Leadership dynamics in which participants shared their individual challenges; 2) Unresolved situations – a topic, issue, friction, problem – in which participants were intensively involved; 3) Exploring your senses, which was geared to stimulating the awareness of the participants' senses and how they are connected to feelings, which in turn stimulates behaviour; 4) Catering and location, for which a professional chef took care of our energy base for a week.[7] I loved the concept.

Early each morning, we had the choice of starting the day with aerobics or jogging. At the end of the exercise session, I admired the brave and the fanatic, who dived into the cold pond, which was probably 2°C to 4°C – far too cold for my liking.

After the morning exercises, we had a good wholesome breakfast – organic porridge – something I had not eaten since I was a kid. The chef – a specialist in macrobiotic food – prepared a different meal each day that was made with ingredients geared towards having a healthy impact on a specific organ. During the course of the week, he had an impact on most of our vital organs. His explanations about the menu were very insightful.

Group sessions in the mornings and evenings took us through the different "dynamics" that Arri describes in his book and how they impact your leadership behaviour. Seated in a circle, we would listen to Arri explain the dynamic of the day. After the introduction, we would discuss in small groups of two or three what it meant for us in both our business and personal lives. A few participants were then asked to share their personal insights with the entire group. This led to some very interesting and sometimes emotional discussions and conversations.

The afternoons were experiential. I was shocked when I first saw the programme agenda – one afternoon, we would dance, and on another, we would sing. If there are two things that I do not like to do they are dancing and singing, for the simple reason that I have absolutely no talent for either of these activities. I was more attracted to the other two afternoons with the martial arts and yoga sessions.

The martial arts session taught me an important lesson. First, the trainer took us through all kinds of boxing and karate exercises. Then, at a certain point, the other participants circled around and pushed against you with thick boxing cushions. Your task was to break out of the circle. They were instructed to antagonize you, so of course you start to fight like mad. After kicking and pushing for a while, you become completely exhausted. There is no energy whatsoever left in your body. Nothing! And then, the trainer begins to provoke you by screaming rude things. To my surprise, I became very angry and despite my exhaustion, I started to hit the trainer really hard. Where had all this energy suddenly come from? The lesson was clear: The human body has a lot of latent energy that you can access if your body, spirit and mind are perfectly aligned.

> **insight**
>
> *The human body has a lot of latent energy that you can access if your body, spirit and mind are perfectly aligned.*

> **insight**
>
> *Be yourself, focus and enjoy what you are doing. Don't worry what others might think about you.*

The dancing, which I had a total misconception about, turned out to be great. It does not matter if others see that your moves are bad and that you are out of sync with the music. What matters is experiencing the vitality that comes from dancing with your partner as one, following each other's movements and being guided by the music. The lesson was clear: Be yourself, focus and enjoy what you are doing. Do not worry what others might think of you and your partner.

A breakthrough: My first appearance on stage as a singer

As it turned out, I knew the music trainer from a leadership event that Arri and I had organized for a large group of food business leaders at Unilever. The trainer – a fun guy – was able to get audiences to do unexpected things. At the Unilever event, he presented himself as a communications professor, sharing a very strange piece of consumer insight with us, while slowly moving in the direction of the importance of singing. Before we realized what was happening, the group of 1,000 leaders was singing – *We did it our way* – to the tune of Frank Sinatra's song – *I did*

Judith's Column

My Song

Judith Buitenhek-van Schooten
Healthcare Psychologist, Therapist & Trainer
The Netherlands

As a psychologist-therapist I have been trained thoroughly to tune into another person and invite, assist and guide him or her to get awareness about and give expression to his or her inner world. It's like tuning a radio, looking for the specific wavelength of the sender and making the connection to bring its message as clear and undistorted as possible on air.

In Frandeux, this is what I did with the participants – functioning as a receiver and a clear as possible tuner for the inner worlds of the participants, supporting them to become aware of what's going on inside and to give expression to it.

As a way of expressing what's going on inside, to me singing has an enormous liberating and transformative power. Especially when it is guided by a master of voice-liberation, such as Jan Kortie, people can rise beyond themselves or more precisely beyond the limitations of their ego to connect to their true self or authentic life force. Life force is the energy of creation and when creative energy becomes liberated, it has a very intense and inspiring effect. This is what

I experienced at the Frandeux voice-liberation workshop when Kees had his turn.

Tuned in to Kees and resonating with him while he was singing, I experienced the liberation of an enormous life force and a wide variety of intense emotions all balled together in the sentences he sang: "Everything vibrates in me, life vibrates in me and I feel free."

The life force that got liberated as Kees expressed himself right from the heart, inspired me to write the poem "Authenticity", transforming all the intense emotions that I had picked up and transmitted during his singing.

"Authenticity" has now turned into one of my favourite songs that I regularly sing and play on my guitar and I feel very grateful to Kees for having inspired me.

Judith has 25 years of experience in working with individuals, couples, parents and groups in different kinds of settings. She is co-trainer in the Genesis Leadership Development Program. Under the name Judith Kiowa she writes poems and songs, and paints.

Authenticity

Everything vibrates in me
I am so happy to be
Flowing with life's energy
Setting my emotions free

My love and pain
My guilt and shame
Hopes and despair
So much to share
My joy and pride
Or sheer delight
My hate and fears
Blind rage and tears

Everything vibrates in me
I am so happy to be
Playing with life's energy
Express itself through me

Let's sing, not fight
Make harmony
Let's sing and
Transform agony
Just use your voice
Creatively
Just be yourself
Authentically

Everything vibrates in me
I am so happy to be
Glowing with life's energy
Living the truth in me

it my way. That memory gave me some reassurance about the afternoon.

But then the inevitable happened in Frandeux. We all had to take turns singing in front of the classroom while the trainer played the piano. The first two participants were brilliant. I decided to go next because I thought it would be best not to have the worst performance at the end. I warned the instructor and the audience about my lack of ability, but I still had to sing. So, I decided to brave it, even though I felt like I was about to take my first bungee jump. My adrenaline was pumping, my eyes were closed and the piano player was whispering some words of encouragement. After a while, I realized that I was singing words that expressed my feelings, my emotions. My body was trembling, but I was happy, really happy. Eventually, I was asked to open my eyes and look at the audience. I could not believe what I saw. The audience had tears in their eyes – they had been emotionally touched by my song. Many questions were going through my mind. What happened? Why? Then I realized I was still singing and I was even using my hands and body to express myself. When I finally stopped, I had been on stage for more than twenty minutes and the group members all came up to hug me. For me, it felt like a miracle. I felt incredibly satisfied that I had been able to get in touch with my inner self – one that I did not know existed.

Arri's Column

Living my authenticity

Arri Pauw
Partner, Genesis Consulting Group
Author of *The Road Within – In Search of Authentic Leadership*
http://genesisconsultinggroup.com

Living my authenticity is a major theme in my life. It gives me joy, when I notice it in me, when I see it happening with human beings around me. The Genesis Leadership Development Program serves as a platform for people who want to join me in that longing. It moves and energizes me to guide participants in the process of self-reflection to grow their awareness of their uncensored capabilities, personal talents and inner **values** and to see them rediscovering the joy and strength of their uniqueness.

When Kees writes about connecting to his authenticity, he refers to the unique combination of qualities and capabilities *inside himself*, and manifesting these *outside himself* – without restraining himself by upfront judgement. I saw it happening with him as I do with other participants of the Leadership weeks. When he was singing, he went away from us, inside himself, to then return and connect as never before. His presence transformed from an anxious expression of, "I will never meet their expectations, so I better get this over with quickly" to a firmly grounded expression of, "I am Kees". Afterwards, initially, he showed surprise, which I can deeply relate to, because it is so alien for most of us to behave free from internalised social conditioning. But next, seeing how it elevated the others, the secret was revealed: *When I behave authentically, it energizes all those around me and has a direct impact.*

Our world, our organisations, our private relations have a love-hate relationship with authenticity. We hire new employees for their unique qualities. Equally, we don't seek the average life-partner, but someone unique to us. However, the moment that the relationship is sealed (labour contract signed, marriage arranged), we define the behaviour we prefer for the other – as the role demands, our organisation defines, our culture prescribes. In turn, they confine themselves to our limitations. We strangle each other's authenticity in order to meet the expectations of the individual and the collective others. Together, we become safely, predictably homogenized. Self-reflection is necessary to regain access to our unique and full range of capabilities, talents and inner values. If we want results beyond the predictable and controllable, we had better start living our authenticity. Growing awareness delivers results!

GENESIS
CONSULTING GROUP

REFLECTIONS

In Chapters 1, 2 and 3, I have highlighted the importance of the creation of balance between work, family and societal activities. In this last chapter, I have illustrated through three different stories how essential it is to look after yourself and ways that you can do this. One essential component is the ability to show your real self

> ### insight
>
> *Leaders who own their behaviour, including their dysfunctional behaviour, are more successful, more passionate and they act according to their inner purpose.*

to your organization – to show that you are a normal human being with emotions and feelings. One should never fall into the trap of thinking that a leader has to be rock solid, hard and just rational. You have to be yourself, your authentic self. You have to allow the people around you to invest time in looking after themselves, and you have to provide the circumstances for self-reflection and self-development.

My experience in Frandeux helped me understand the real meaning of authenticity. Leaders face constant pressure to deliver results, and this pressure can sometimes end in not being true to oneself. Leaders who own their behaviour, including their dysfunctional behaviour, are more successful, more passionate and they act according to their inner purpose. They are less superficial, and they will be admired and respected more because they are honest, human and real.

CEOs, future leaders and others involved in managing large groups of individuals are well advised to get off their daily treadmills at the office and spend time with themselves to understand their motives and their inner truth, purpose, drivers and talents. If you are able to do this, you will become more authentic rather than a caricature of yourself. As a result, you will be a more effective leader because you will be able to mobilize people to take on difficult tasks and you will be able to access the energy you need to achieve your plans and deliver your results.

> ### insight
>
> *CEOs, future leaders and others involved in managing large groups of individuals are well advised to get off their daily treadmills at the office and spend time with themselves to understand their motives and their inner truth, purpose, drivers and talents.*

Notes

[1] Senge, Peter, C. Otto Scharmer, Joseph Jaworski and Betty Sue Flowers. *Presence: An Exploration of Profound Change in People, Organizations, and Society.* New York: Currency/Doubleday, 2004.

[2] By Oriah © Mountain Dreaming from the book The Invitation published by HarperONE, San Francisco, 1999. All rights reserved. www.oriah.org

[3] Jaworski, Joseph & Katherine Parrot (Eds.) *U-Process Book of Readings.* Beverly, MA: Generon Consulting, 2005.

[4] www.generoninternational.com (accessed 6 December 2010).

[5] Jaworski, Joseph & Katherine Parrot (Eds.) *U-Process Book of Readings.* Beverly, MA: Generon Consulting, 2005. (Generon now uses a more advanced model of the U-Process which is called "The U-Process for Heuristic Discovery"; see www.generoninternational.com.)

[6] Berentsen, Laurens. "Kees van der Graaf: 'Ik verloor mijn prioriteiten uit het oog.'" *Het Financieele Dagblad*, Zaterdag 8 maart 2008.

[7] Pauw, Arri. *The Road Within: In Search of Authentic Leadership Behavior.* AuthorHouse, 2010.

[8] http://genesisleadership.org/page.php?pageID=122 (accessed 17 January 2011).

Final thoughts

5

During the course of my 32-year career at Unilever, I had the pleasure of working in 15 different jobs in five countries (the US, UK, Spain, Switzerland and the Netherlands) with 21 different bosses and 15 great assistants. I visited 61 countries and for the three years that I was responsible for the Far East, while based in Rotterdam, I was permanently jetlagged from racking up 100,000 air miles travelling back and forth. In the last 20 years, I have taken 2,018 flights and have been away from home on business for more than 2,200 nights, of which Renée was with me for only about 50.

Along the way, I have had many defining moments – some unexpected; others orchestrated – that have helped me discover my true purpose, my values, my beliefs and ultimately my personal balance.

MY NEW LIFE

When I wrote this title for the first time, I immediately had second thoughts. Another title that I have sometimes used when talking to people at Unilever who were having difficulty accepting the fact that they were being made redundant was, "There is

> **insight**
>
> *If you are not enjoying your job, be willing to consider the alternatives. It may be hard to imagine, but the world is full of possibilities and opportunities waiting to be taken.*

life after Unilever". If you ever find yourself in a position where you are not enjoying your job anymore, you should not feel that you have to attach yourself to one and only one employer. It may be hard to imagine, but the world is full of possibilities and opportunities waiting to be taken. But you have to have an open mind and be willing to consider the alternatives.

When I took my early retirement, I was warned not to be too hasty in accepting any new roles. Initially, all was calm. Together with the family, we went on a long holiday to China that included the Olympics in Beijing and other parts of China. After returning from this fantastic journey, I accepted the Executive-in-Residence role at IMD. This seemed to be a once -in-a- lifetime opportunity.

Soon after, all kinds of big and small opportunities came my way. Fortunately

though, I remembered the wise advice from my "pensionado" friends. I was choosy, but looking back now, three years later, perhaps not choosy enough. I have probably accepted too many roles. I am busy again and my agenda is looking a little full. But – and it's a big but – I enjoy what I am doing, and if I cease to enjoy it, I will remove myself in an orderly fashion from the responsibility. I am in control of my agenda – nobody else is setting it for me. And perhaps most importantly, I have a common purpose for everything I do.

Let me explain. I love business and the sensation of seeing results. That is where I probably have some skills and competences. I also love engaging with young managers and future leaders. By sharing my experiences – my mistakes and my successes – I hope they will

... in this chapter

- **My new life**
- **Insights**
- **Behaviours to avoid**
- **Ten steps towards total personal balance**
- **My dream**

learn something. Standing in front of an MBA class is one of the most inspiring experiences I have had in the last five years. They are so bright, so eager to learn, so critical and ask such good questions. I really have to give myself fully to make an impact. I get a lot of energy from those sessions and, best of all, I sense it is mutual.

In short, I enjoy teaching, lecturing and sharing my experiences, mirroring, writing and doing supervisory board work for select companies and organizations that contribute to the betterment of society. My pension income is more than sufficient to support a decent life, so any income that these activities generate is either donated by the organizations involved or by me personally in the form of a five-year grant to the FSHD Foundation. The beauty of this is that my donations are fully tax deductible under the Dutch tax system so the Foundation gets the gross amount of the income before taxes. In a way, I have created a virtuous circle. In order to find a cure for FSHD, we need more financial means for research, which I can help generate by working a bit more and transferring the revenues to the Foundation. Getting closer to a cure stimulates me to work harder on the things I enjoy most – contributing to the creation of better future leaders and a better world.

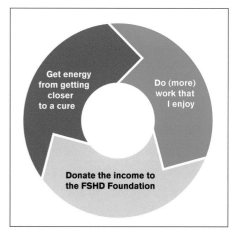

My virtuous circle

Diederik

Soon after starting my Executive-in-Residence role at IMD, I noticed that my second oldest son, Diederik, was having difficulty getting started on writing his final thesis for his finance studies at the University of Amsterdam. St. Nicolas day, which is celebrated on December 5 in the Netherlands, was approaching. On this occasion, we exchange presents and poems. By tradition, you can put whatever message you want in the poems that you write, so I made a few joking remarks in Diederik's poem about the speed at which he was going through his studies. I also suggested that he come to Lausanne, to IMD, to write his final paper in a quiet, stimulating, academic environment. I had an apartment with a spare bedroom close to IMD. He read the poem aloud, in front of the entire family including his girlfriend. When he finished reading the poem, he immediately said, "That is a great idea. I will take you up on the offer!" His girlfriend was a bit shocked that he did not consult her, but she also saw the advantages.

And so it happened. He moved into my apartment in Lausanne. We shared my desk at IMD. He was able to access IMD's resources, which are limitless and enabled him to get all the materials he needed. He was also able to meet with research associates and professors on a couple of occasions for consultation.

Every morning, we would get up at the same time, go to the bakery around the corner to buy some fresh bread and walk to IMD. We worked at our desk until we were satisfied with our progress, then a couple of times per week we would head to the IMD gym. Each evening we shopped and prepared a simple supper together.

It was a privilege to have my 26-year-old son all to myself for such a long period of time. How many parents can say that! It would not have happened if I had continued to work full time with Unilever. Diederik and I both enjoyed our months together – it was a sort of reconnection. Renée was able to join us for a week of skiing in Chamonix. And his girlfriend was able to visit once while I was back in Holland.

INSIGHTS: THE BIG THEMES

While several insights have been highlighted throughout the book, I would like to share with you the most significant ones, which I have organized around three important themes: Develop yourself constantly, act responsibly and develop your social skills.

Develop yourself constantly

Balance and rebalance

Lead a holistic life. Beyond work, spend quality time with your family and have at least one real activity in the community. Give yourself fully to all three – it is not either/or – it is and, and, and. The energy you get from each of the different activities in which you are involved will sometimes help you deal with setbacks in one area or another.

If you want to stay balanced under all circumstances, you have to stay in control of your agenda. As soon as others start to control your agenda, you quickly lose control of your life. It is so easy to get totally absorbed by your job. If you are passionate about the products and services, your company is offering, and if you are really committed to delivering results, the business will start to dominate your life. You will find yourself working harder and harder, with more and more hours being put into the fulfilment of your business mission. Family life and societal activities will suffer. There is only one way to deal with this. Be clear about your top three to five priorities. As mentioned, take all appointments that are not directly related to your top priorities out of your calendar. You will be amazed how much "nonsense" you will find in your calendar, and how much space you can create by being focused.

Finally, be aware that there is not one static point of total balance. You need to permanently rebalance and adapt yourself to a new mix of circumstances.

Adapt your leadership style

Different situations and issues require different approaches. You will have noticed from the different stories that I adapted my leadership style to the situation of the moment. At times, I have been directive and have taken the ultimate decision; at other times, I have acted as a catalyst for the team to reach certain conclusions so that they take ownership of the decision. In choosing the most appropriate style – from dictatorial to participative – I recommend going with your gut instinct, which is based on the collective wisdom you have gained from your experiences in life.

Be authentic

My best advice – **know yourself, be yourself and show yourself**. Authenticity is one of the best recipes for success for a leader. Textbooks often provide you with lots of ground rules on how to behave. But people will sense immediately when your actions and behaviours are not genuine.

> **My favourite books[1]**
> - Who Moved My Cheese?
> - Getting to Yes
> - The Starfish and the Spider
> - The Ice Cream Maker
> - Small is Beautiful

Leaders can be more authentic when their personal values and purpose in life are aligned with their organizations' values. These conditions create an environment in which a leader can credibly lead with purpose and passion and execute power through inspiration. Leaders who "own" their behaviour, including their dysfunctional behaviour, are more successful, more passionate and they act according to their inner purpose. They are less superficial, and they will be respected and admired because they are honest, human and above all *real*. Do not be afraid to show your emotions, your passions and your strongly held beliefs.

Keep learning

You are never too old to learn. Embrace the concept of lifelong learning. Once you have completed your formal education, participated in several leadership courses, racked up years of experience and read numerous management books, you may start to think that you know it all. However, what you should realize is how little you know. It is only when you begin to master the challenges you are facing, through true listening, observing and digesting, that you start to master your role. Through this process, you will mature and ultimately become respected for your wisdom. You should learn from your mistakes, from your friends and your colleagues, and you should learn from the leaders you admire. I did not have one single leader, but I learnt many things from different individuals.

Take time to reflect

If you ever get the chance to participate in a vision quest (see Chapter 4 – The Montana retreat), do not hesitate – do it. But if that is not possible, you can also do the following: Disappear for a full day into nature. Leave your watch, your mobile phone and your BlackBerry at home. Take lots of water, a pencil and an empty notebook. Leave very early in the morning and find your preferred place in nature – a deserted beach, a forest, the mountains – a place where you can avoid running into people, or at least having to talk to them. Walk for quite a while, until you see your dream spot. You must love it. Sit down, a good distance away from any footpath and just relax. If you know how to meditate, then do it. If not, don't worry. A long walk can have the same calming effect, as long as there is NO contact with people. Then ask yourself the following related questions: Do I enjoy what I am doing? Is this what I intended to do with my life? Is this the legacy I want to leave behind? Am I

Leaders I admire

In the IMD Global CEO Center: Leading in a Connected Future research project, IMD Professor Tom Malnight and I have asked several hundred current and future leaders who they admire as leaders. Many have one clear role model. A few admire a set of individuals for different reasons – I belong to this group. Following are the leaders I admire and the reasons why:

Job van der Graaf(†) My Father	For the way he subtly directed me through my first career moves.
Professor Kreiken (†) University of Twente	For his marketing skills.
Eric Guit (†) Marketing Manager Calvé-de Betuwe	For his creativity.
Victor Aranguren Former Chairman Frigo Spain	For his calm and authoritative leadership style.
Jan Peelen Former Board Member Unilever	For his intellectual breadth and the speed at which he thinks.
Peter Brabeck-Letmathe Chairman and Former CEO of Nestlé	For the way he articulated Nestlé's long-term vision.
Morris Tabaksblat Former CEO of Unilever	For his authority and his care for the individual.
Kofi Annan Former Secretary-General of the United Nations	For his contribution to the world and his ability to fill a room.
Barack Obama President of the United States of America	For his charisma.
Louis van Gaal Former Coach of the Dutch Football team currently Head Coach of Bayern Munich	For his perfection in delivering results and for the way he deals with the press.
Peter Bakker CEO of TNT	For what he and his entire organization did for the World Food Programme.
Bill Gates Chairman of Microsoft & **Ted Turner** Chairman of Turner Enterprises Inc.	For the large philanthropic donations they make to improve the health and wellbeing of humankind.

in control of my destiny? Make notes if you want. By taking time out for deep personal reflection and asking yourself these questions, you can discover your real sense of purpose. This will enable you to reach that point where your spirit, mind and body become perfectly aligned.

Stay fit
Look after your yourself – physically, emotionally and spiritually. Train, eat well and build in time for relaxation.

Learn to trust your gut.
Your instincts are very often right. Learn to listen to them. When your intuition tells you that a certain decision is wrong, despite all rational arguments, go with your gut feeling and find a palatable way to explain the reasons why.

Act responsibly
Care!
Care for your people, care for your business, care for society and care for your family and friends. Be available, make time for all those people who want to see you to share something with you or get your opinion or advice. Be approachable. Ensure that your PAs or other assistants do not overprotect you. In doing so, they may end up isolating you. You have to want to listen to the reality around you. You have to be interested in other people.

I often hear senior executives saying that their families are supportive and

---

Pernette's Column

Leadership requires energy and a clear mind

Pernette Osinga
Personal Trainer & Co-founder
HeartWork – www.heart-work.nl

Survival in the business world requires a certain level of fitness. The crushing workload, family and society demands are all pulling you in different directions. On top of that, there are traffic delays, jet lag and numerous other hurdles to deal with on a daily basis. Leadership requires energy and a clear mind. A fit body is a must – not only does it give you the stamina to deal with your conflicting demands, but it also gives you clarity so that you can make the difficult decisions without hesitation.

Kees = energy. He gives energy and reflects energy. Always dedicated, whether it's 6 o'clock in the morning or 10 o'clock at night, Kees continuously strives to get the best out of himself and the people around him.

---

understanding of their need to work hard. In response, I always say: "Careful – like your bank account, you need to keep things balanced. If you become overdrawn, your bank manager might suddenly decide to cut you off!"

Take your full vacation entitlement
Spend it with the family. Try to arrange your schedule in such a way that you can be at every special occasion for the kids – the first ballet or music performance, their football matches on the weekend, the parent-teacher meetings at school. If

posted in a new country, be sensitive to the feelings and emotions of your family. Make brave decisions when necessary, even if it means ending your career with your current employer.

Remember the important personal situations of your direct reports. Give them a call at a crucial moment. Work with HR to anticipate the consequences of a difficult family situation for both the individual and the business. If it proves necessary, consider a job move for the individual; at least be creative in offering small gestures that will have a big impact, such as Roy Brown's reaction when I asked for unpaid leave (see Chapter 1 – Spieren voor Spieren). Do not be afraid to share your own personal matters with your superiors.

Champion what really matters

As a leader, you have to be the passionate champion of all those activities and projects that really matter. The entire organization must see you as being absolutely consistent in all of your behaviours in driving, supporting and facilitating the chosen results. To get the desired results, you have to give space and empower and stimulate the project leaders. Support your people in completing their tasks and be very considerate when it comes to their personal circumstances. When the desired results have been reached, give those responsible a lot of public recognition. By doing this you get the best that people have to give.

Take responsibility

Select the right CSR initiative to demonstrate that the organization is taking its impact on the environment and society seriously. Give back what you have taken from society. Do this in terms of reliable, good quality products and services, but also in terms of care for the world in which we live. Contribute to creating a better world and saving the planet. As Unilever says: "Little steps – big differences". Doing nothing to save our planet is not an option!

Use CSR to engage, motivate and inspire your people. If you really want to reap the benefits of your CSR initiatives, ensure that, in principle, all of your employees participate in the project. Not by donating money, but through active engagement – using their brains and their hearts. Create an emotional bond. Aim for a long-term commitment. The project should be aligned with the core capabilities of your organization. As a result, you will get the tangible and non-tangible business benefits and the workforce will become more energized and motivated than ever before. It will also be very insightful to notice that your people have many more capabilities than just doing a nice job for you.

Develop your social skills

Embrace the power of teams

Trust is at the heart of building effective teams, where people give their very best and put the team's success ahead of their own. Without trust, you can forget about delivering exceptional results. Trust, however, is something you must build and earn over time by treating, rewarding and recognizing people in a fair and consistent way. An effective leader gives people the space – freedom within a framework – to do their jobs, trusts them to do well, allows them to learn from their mistakes and is generous in rewarding them (both financially and non-financially). Trust also means sharing confidential information to ensure that the individuals understand the context of certain decisions. When team members know they can trust each other, the team becomes unbeatable.

Organize an annual, offsite *team reflection* event with all your direct reports to address the following: How are we doing – what went well and what could we do better? Ensure you do not just talk about business results. Spend an equal amount of time on the softer issues, such as team chemistry and individual and collective behavioural issues. Allow space for hidden interpersonal issues to surface and deal with them appropriately.

Types of events

- **Building corporate culture.** Agreeing on and sharing vision, mission and values. Agreeing on acceptable and non-acceptable behaviours.
- **Setting strategic direction** and **developing must-win battles**.
- **Celebrating success.** When the group has over-delivered on targets, you **should always plan a celebration to recognize the significant** contribution it has made.
- **Communicating** really important messages/decisions.
- **Teambuilding.**

Make the team feel important. They matter to you. By taking the team away from the office to develop the strategy, choose the must-win battles and develop plans to address major discontinuities, you send the message that you value their input and their challenges. Let them know you are not afraid of constructive conflict, but that you insist on mutual respect. The key is bringing the team together. Together, you know more, together you develop better solutions and together you care for the collective successes.

The CO₄ Model

1. <u>C</u>ompelling need. Create a compelling need for change, a so-called burning platform. Nobody likes change. Change is associated with fear. You can overcome this by making it crystal clear that there is no other alternative.
2. <u>Co</u>-create. Together, develop options, scenarios and alternatives. Reach a shared vision of the future. Choose the recommended way forward together. This will create full ownership of the chosen way forward.
3. <u>Co</u>mmit. Demand the full commitment of the team. It is best to earn this through a process of engagement and involvement.
4. <u>Co</u>mmunicate, communicate, communicate. Use all available media, all occasions and all possibilities to reach out in a passionate way to the entire organization. Ensure the message is clear, consistent and usable by all team members.

Drive change, be courageous

There is a constant need for change. Not changing means standing still, suffering from complacency and losing out to competition. Continuous improvement is the name of the game. Adapt yourself to new circumstances and innovate. Small incremental steps will not get you where you want to be. It is better to take bold decisions and drive the implementation quickly and pragmatically throughout the entire organization. Ensure there is agreement around what you are promising and make sure to deliver what you promise. Once a consensus has been reached, stop the debate and implement with rigor. Today, I often use the CO₄ model to describe the four key steps in driving change in an organization.

Do not be afraid to make bold decisions. If you want to reduce complexity, go for daring targets; do not fall into the trap of "death by a thousand cuts". Do it once, do it well and ensure it lasts.

Make clever use of special events

When well organized, an event can do wonders. It can have real impact, bring alignment and create emotional bonds between individuals. Events should be milestones, and should always serve a purpose. Every event should be inspiring, engaging, involving and memorable.

Communicate

It sounds so simple, but it is so difficult, and it is always left to the end as almost an afterthought. It is so important to really prepare a good communications plan. You have to embed it in your thinking and behaviour. You must give it the highest priority. Every time you and your team have reached a conclusion, you must design an adequate communications programme and focus on a small set of key messages. Any meeting that does not end with a discussion and agreement of the key messages is a bad meeting. You should agree who will deliver the messages and which audiences should be addressed, what will be done in writing and what will be done in person and which media and communication vehicles will be used. Remember the importance of repetition. Messages only come across if they are received in a compelling and consistent way. It does not matter whether you are sick and tired of telling the same message over and over again. What matters is that you reach your target audience and that they start to move in the desired direction. What matters is that the messages reach the minds and the hearts of the individuals they are intended for and that they get internalized. Make impact. Use unexpected ways to get attention.

BEHAVIOURS TO AVOID

Some business leaders have certain characteristics that really irritate and upset me. These are probably the root cause of the problems we are now facing in the economy, and they are also why some large multinationals have difficulty dealing with their negative perceptions and images.

1. Greed

This is at the heart of most issues – leaders who always want more and more money for themselves. Salaries are becoming far too high and bonuses (particularly in financial services) are outrageous. This bonus culture leads to the wrong decisions and the wrong behaviours. Industry leaders should come together and take proactive action before the legislators come with unworkable solutions.

2. Selfishness

Celebrity CEOs who appear in the press too often and put their own interests ahead of the interests of the firm often develop superiority complexes. With their know-it-all attitudes, they tend not to listen to others, which results in them becoming more and more isolated.

3. Operating from an ivory tower

Too often, I see leaders who are too remote from the reality of the marketplace and the real business. As a result, their information is based on historical experience and, therefore, it is dated. They have become untouchable and out of touch.

4. Listening to the wrong people

Some CEOs are surrounded by a large number of staff who "protect" them from being influenced by the front-liners in the organization. However, the front-line people are often more experienced and insightful than the armies of consultants that are hired to help the company gain a so-called external perspective.

5. Blaming the predecessor

The predecessor is always blamed for the current state of affairs. This makes it possible for the CEO to clear the decks at huge costs and then get full credit for the restructuring, which shows real progress for the next two years.

6. Short-term outlook

Too often, CEOs are under pressure to deliver on quarterly expectations for the financial analysts. This leads to optimizing the quarter, rather than driving sustainable results. There is a simple reason for this general lack of appreciation for sustainable performance – the investors. There are two types of investors – the opportunists who want volatility and love "news" because this creates movement in the stock prices, which is where they earn their money and their ridiculous bonuses. The other type – the real investors – buy a stock because they believe in the future prospects of the business; they behave like owners of the firm and stimulate management to deliver long-term results.

7. Putting shareholder value maximization ahead of stakeholder value creation

It is still a common belief in certain circles and even among some faculty of well-known business schools that the only purpose of a business is to maximize profits. But the time has come for leaders to realize that you do not simply take without giving anything back. Leaders should act more responsibly in the areas of sustainability and social responsibility. The world in which we live, the planet that we occupy, will be ruined if we do not change this attitude and, instead, focus on total value creation, which satisfies the needs of a multi-stakeholder configuration.

TEN STEPS TOWARDS TOTAL PERSONAL BALANCE

I would like to point out that it is impossible to consistently achieve total balance. As leaders, we have to think in terms of dynamic balance rather than static balance. There will always be forces that will throw us out of balance, and we have to accept that from time to time, as long as we recognize it and are prepared to constantly rebalance our priorities. It is not a matter of phases in life; it is the ability to constantly find a new equilibrium. And relationships can play an important role in this – we all need help rebalancing our lives on occasion and in turn we can all provide help to those around us. My hope is that the combination of the stories I have shared with you in this book and the following 10 steps will serve

as a wake-up call to step back and take the time to create your own personal balance.

1. Define your real purpose in life

When I talk about purpose, I mean real purpose – your deeper purpose – not just

defining your personal objectives. Think about what you want your legacy to be. What do you want to be remembered for? What do you stand for? The answers to these questions do not come overnight – they take time – time alone with yourself. You need to ponder, reflect, think and rethink what you want your life to

---

My main purpose in life

My main purpose in life, as I discovered at the executive retreat in 1995 with C.K. Prahalad (Chapter 1) is to find a cure for FSHD and to support Renée, Bart, Diederik and Michiel in making their lives as enjoyable as possible.

Next to that, I want to contribute to creating a better world by increasing the awareness of the up-and-coming generation of future leaders of the importance of taking responsibility for the impact business is having and should be having on the environment.

---

27 things I want to do before I die

One of the exercises change agents and consultants often conduct during a session to create alignment in a team is ask you to write down 27 things you want to do before you die. The time they give you is always short, so the list is never complete or completely thought through. What it does, however, is establish a list that you can share with other team members. The lists tell a lot about the individuals and they become the launching pad for creating alignment among team members.

Since I first created my list, I have toyed with it, tweaked it, grouped it under related headings. It has now grown beyond 27 things and it is not in order of priority, but it does provide some good insights into what drives and motivates me. Below are a few of the things on my list:

- Sailing my own boat down the Belgian River Maas, through the French canals and down the Rhone to the Mediterranean, through the Black Sea and then back home up the Danube.
- Attend the farewell tour of the Rolling Stones.
- Be a buddy to Bart wherever and whenever he wishes me to do so.
- Organize the Winter Olympics in the Netherlands together with Sarajevo.
- Meet "admired leaders", such as Kofi Annan, to learn from them for the benefit of the younger generation.

represent. Once you have found it: write it down and keep it close to you. You might want to share it with a few people who are dear to you. Confirmation and positive encouragement are great helps.

2. Define your personal values

What really matters to you? Once you have defined your values you have to ensure that your behaviour is consistent with them. Only then will you be perceived as being authentic.

3. Identify your top five priorities

Once you know what really matters to you, you can start to develop a plan to fulfil your life's mission. The plan should include no more than five sharply defined

Sandy's Column

The magic of dynamic balance

Sandy Ogg
Operating Partner, Portfolio Operations Group
The Blackstone Group – www.blackstone.com
Former Chief Human Resources Officer of Unilever

Much has been written about corporate social responsibility and work-life balance. These are two very important ideas that have captured the imagination and energy of many forward-looking organizations. Until now, I was not aware of anyone who had written about (much less practised) the magic of "dynamically balancing" one's energy among family, a major corporation and society in a systematic way.

Corporate social responsibility has emerged as a way of resolving the conflict that can arise at the point where a corporation and the society in which it operates intersect. Forward-thinking organizations with visionary leaders like Unilever's Paul Polman say that we must not "steal from future generations". Organizations will simply not attain the "right to grow" if they cannot do it in a sustainable way.

Operating within a framework of responsibility is becoming increasingly important for organizations that want to

attract and retain the very best people. At a recent football match that I attended, I asked the woman next to me where she worked. She said, "I don't tell people anymore; I am ashamed by all the negative stuff that has appeared in the press". She later told me that she worked for one of the most respected firms on Wall Street!

Not only do employees want to be part of organizations that behave responsibly, they also want their organizations to give them the opportunity to live a full life whilst pursuing a fulfilling career. The best organizations are working to do just that. At Unilever, we are experimenting with innovative "agile working" practices to help our employees find ways to navigate the blurring lines between work and life. Advanced video conferencing, for example, reduces expensive travel costs and allows employees to spend more time at home – a win-win.

Progress in these areas requires a group of committed leaders who believe that their responsibilities extend beyond the walls of organizations; otherwise, the initiatives stall. Unilever is working to establish a performance-oriented leadership culture to support these efforts.

The idea that Kees puts forward in this book – the thought (and practice) of "dynamically balancing" family responsibilities, serving a major corporation and caring for society is a compelling proposition. Through his examples, he illustrates how one can be true to oneself as well as one's family, work and society – what a powerful thought!

priorities for the next 5 to 10 years. Write them down and reread them 24 hours later to see if they still feel right. If necessary, adjust them, but ask yourself why this is necessary. It could be important to go back to your purpose and value statements.

4. Make courageous decisions

Once you have decided on your deeper purpose, your values and your priorities, you face a moment of truth. You must clear your agenda of all the things that do not fit. If you can do this, then you will be perfectly aligned and perfectly happy. If there is a deviation, you will probably have to make some adjustments to your agenda to create more time for your priorities. If there is a total misalignment, it is time to step back and re-evaluate what you want out of life. This requires some deep reflection about yourself, your relationships, your job and so on. Talk to the people in your life – your partner, your coach, your boss – and if you still feel that you cannot align your agenda with your priorities, then perhaps it is time to take the brave step of removing yourself from your job. Agree with your boss on the best way to do this, and keep in mind that there is a life after your current employer.

5. Deal with the root cause of the problem

Staying true to your purpose and focusing on your top five priorities is not easy. You will encounter all kinds of challenges along the way. My advice – follow a Chinese

---

> # My values
>
> - **Care** – for my family, my friends, the planet and the people on it.
> - **Take responsibility** – for my decisions and for those areas that have been assigned to my charge. This requires courage so as not to shy away from making difficult decisions.
>
> # My beliefs
>
> - **Integrity** is at the heart of being a trustworthy and credible leader.
> - **Deliver on your promises**, and only promise what you can deliver. If you cannot deliver on your promises, analyse why and inform your superiors about what happened and more importantly, what you are doing in terms of corrective measures.
> - **Keep things simple**. We all tend to have a fantastic ability to make things complex – we love to make things complicated. In my view, a leader needs to be relentless in weeding out unnecessary complexity and become world class at managing the necessary complexity – Kees's law.

---

medicine philosophy. [3] When Tom Malnight and I talked to a number of Chinese CEOs during our research project, they told us that when they are facing an issue or a dilemma, rather than treat the symptoms, they search for and address the root cause.

6. Get inspiration from exceptional individuals

There are a lot of truly exceptional people in the world. Look around you. Look for people you admire not only for their achievements but also how they achieved them. Talk to them. Learn from them. Seek their support and let them energize you. I have been fortunate to have been inspired by some truly exceptional people. They have taught me things about myself and about life in general. Each one has had a

message – many of which I have described in this book – that has energized me: Peggy Dulany (importance of partnerships in philanthropy), Joseph Jaworski (synchronicity), Annie McKee (leadership), Paul Vincent (unconditional love), Tom Malnight (management of change), Arri Pauw (authenticity) and C.K. Prahalad (foresight).

Needless to say, I have also been inspired by my family – my parents, my sons and my wife – for their determination, commitment and love.

7. Get fit and stay fit

Leaders need endurance. Top physical condition is necessary to sustain endurance. To get into shape, you need to train, exercise and eat a balanced diet.

Tuitert: An inspiration

Mark Tuitert celebrating his 1500 m Gold medal in the 2010 Vancouver Olympics.[5]

Top athletes provide tremendous inspiration for me. I get very emotional when an individual or a team wins a championship or a medal — Mark Tuitert for example.

At the 2010 Vancouver Olympics, Tuitert, a veteran Dutch speed skater, was racing for a medal in the 1,500-meter sprint. The hot favourite to win was American Shani Davis. Tuitert had not been on the podium for a long time due to a number of setbacks and disappointments over the years. But when you saw him come on the ice in Vancouver, you knew he was ready for something great. His eyes, his posture, his movements – he looked strong and full of confidence. He was ready to conquer the world and he did. He started fast – too fast in the eyes of the experts. But he was able to keep up the momentum and the strength to win the race, set the best time and win Olympic Gold. Sheer joy replaced all the frustrations and disappointments of the past.

Later he explained that he knew that this was going to be his day despite the fact that the conditions were not good. The ice was his. He felt strong and he was in control – his spirit, mind and body were perfectly aligned. A fantastic source of inspiration.

Watch it on YouTube

Speed skating Men 1500 m Gold Vancouver 2010

Some people can do it by themselves; others need help. I engaged a personal trainer to help me stick to my regimen. What matters is that you develop a routine that works for you and then stick to it. I find it helpful to set targets for myself by participating in organized events, such as a 1/8 triathlon or a bicycle race. Exercise, along with a balanced diet, will help you maintain the right weight and body mass index (BMI), as well as allow you to indulge in some of the special things you enjoy, keeping in mind that moderation is key.

Finally, do not forget your mental fitness. Figure out what relaxes you, whether it is meditation, yoga, long walks on the beach or staring at a fish aquarium. The key is to develop rituals that help keep you mentally fit.

8. Be organized and disciplined

Focusing on your priorities and maintaining your physical and mental fitness takes extreme organization and discipline. No matter how busy you are, you need to schedule some non-negotiable time for must-do activities. In my case, I scheduled a round of golf every Sunday morning at 8 am. Do not be lured away from your must-do activities, as you will only be fooling yourself. This requires setting tough targets and then organizing yourself in such a way that you can achieve them thereby making time for your priorities and your fitness.

9. Recharge your batteries

We all need breaks. There is a limit to how much stress a person can take. Always take your vacation entitlement. No one will thank you for not taking your breaks. It is important for you and for your family to take time out to bond and to create long-lasting memories together. Leave "out-of-office" messages saying that you do not have access to e-mail or voicemail. However, if it is impossible to be completely out of touch with your office during your vacation, schedule a maximum of two short, unobtrusive breaks during the day to check and respond to messages.

I also learnt that taking extra vitamins the week before your vacation starts helps you overcome the changes in your metabolism that seem to manifest in an "off" day around the third day of your vacation.

Finally, if the pressures of your job drain your energy, try tapping into other sources of energy to help you cope – your partner, your children or your societal activities.

10. Evaluate

Once a year, take a day for yourself and assess your performance on the first nine steps of this action plan. How did you do? Are you living up to the promises you made to yourself? Hopefully you can pat yourself on the back and say, "Well done my friend". But, most likely, there is room for improvement.

Reflect, rethink and understand the reasons for the deviations from the original plan. It is possible you have fallen back into old behaviours and habits. This is often an indication that you are not in control of your own agenda. In this case, do what the Chinese CEOs told us they do during our CEO interviews. When faced with a problem, zero-base, go back to square one. Discover what went wrong and why. Then, take whatever courageous action you have to take to regain your total personal balance.

Recharge your batteries

The BlackBerry

At one point, I became so fed up with people using their BlackBerry smartphones during meetings that I prepared an e-mail to all participants of the next meeting. The e-mail, which was not sent until the meeting, told the participants that I had noticed that they seemed to be more interested in their e-mail than in the meeting. I went on to give them the choice of leaving the meeting or switching off their smartphones. Once the meeting had been convened, I noticed several of my team members using their BlackBerry smartphones. At that moment, I pressed the send button. The fanatics in the room saw the red light flashing and immediately checked their messages. I could see their faces turning red as they looked at me and switched off their BlackBerry smartphones. It was the last time I had a problem with people checking their messages in a meeting.

I told this story to several people and it gained a life of its own within Unilever. The truth is it never happened, but it did the trick for me.

Mark's Column

Walking the talk

Mark Rutte
Prime Minister of the Kingdom of the Netherlands

By 2001 I had been working at Unilever for over eight years. That year I got involved in organising 15 workshops that were being held in the elegant *Château des Prés d'Ecoublay* for each of the company's 15 divisions and business groups. The goal was to turn a firm that was very profitable but not growing into one that would be both very profitable and growing. That called for a major transformation of its corporate culture. In those days, Unilever was an archipelago of isolated national organizations that barely worked together. Its culture was risk-averse, and far too much time was wasted on internal politics.

Tom Malnight, a professor at IMD business school, and I worked closely with Kees to fine-tune the workshops so they were just the way Kees wanted them. At the time, Kees had recently taken charge of Unilever's Ice Cream and Frozen Foods Europe business group. The group's 50 senior managers from the different countries and head office would all be there. Tom and I soon realized that Kees was an outstanding leader. It was up to us to make the most of his talents.

1. **Kees is profoundly values-driven.** This made the second evening of the workshop, when he shared his life story with the group, unforgettable. He spoke without any reserve about his deepest convictions, his worries, what he had been through. And he talked about his family and his determination to find a treatment for his son's illness. He became a role model for us all, helping to create a new culture of openness and respect. He did this not by pontificating but by humbly telling us his own story.

2. **He is capable of deep listening and genuine, creative dialogue.** This is what ensured that his encounter with his new team, earlier that day in a Turkish tent, would have such an impact. He confronted them with their hypocrisy in grumbling about a strategy that all of them had earlier committed to. After lunch, however, he explained what he was doing and showed that he was open to what they had to say. That moment proved to be a turning point.

3. **He has tremendous drive and an enormous amount of energy.** This made the end of the workshop on Friday a remarkable experience. He began working on his closing statement at five in the morning. He went back over all the material the group had produced in the course of the week. The flipcharts told the whole story. Using every inch of space, the 50 participants had told their own stories: the concerns and expectations they had come with, the things they needed to do more of and the things they needed to do less of, and the must-win battles they saw ahead. Kees moved between those flipchart sheets, which were arranged to form a cockpit around the group. Everyone stood up and followed him. He put into words everything that had happened that week. His team left Ecoublay with a strategy, with a purpose, and with Kees firmly established as their leader.

And that was the key lesson of the week. That kind of workshop, where culture and strategy go hand in hand, only makes sense with a leader who does the facilitating himself, uses the consultants only as support, and is capable of winning the hearts and minds of his team.

MY DREAM: TO CONTRIBUTE TO THE CREATION OF A BETTER WORLD THROUGH THIS BOOK

The challenges of the future are immense. The social and environmental challenges alone are well known and numerous. To face this new world, we need leaders who want to grow in more responsible ways. This means that leaders need to rethink some fundamental questions – why we exist, where we should focus and how we can act differently. The world needs authentic leaders with a deep sense of purpose, vision and courage who can inspire their teams to perform miracles so that the world might benefit.

My dream is that the stories, insights and action plans that I have shared in this book will inspire those who read it to develop themselves in new directions to become the highly effective and responsible leaders that the future so badly needs. We need leaders with their hearts in the right place, leaders who care about others and the world in which we live – fighting injustice and helping the underprivileged. Leaders who do away with greed and ridiculous bonuses and who put sustainability ahead of maximizing short-term shareholder value. Leaders who assign equal importance to stakeholders and shareholders. Leaders who inspire others to reach their full potential without abusing their power base.

I hope that this book is seen as an enjoyable and good learning experience for current and future leaders. I have enjoyed writing it and all proceeds will go to the FSHD Foundation – a true win-win.

Notes

[1] Johnson, Spencer.*Who Moved My Cheese*? London: Vermilion, 1999.

Fisher, Roger and William Ury with Bruce Patton (Ed.) *Getting to Yes: Negotiating Agreement without Giving In*. New York: Penguin, 1991.

Brafman, Ori and Rod A. Beckstrom. *The Starfish and the Spider: The Unstoppable Power of Leaderless Organizations*. New York: Portfolio, 2006.

Chowdhury, Subir. *The Ice Cream Maker: An Inspiring Tale about Making Quality The Key Ingredient in Everything You Do*. New York: Currency/Doubleday, 2005.

Schumacher, E.F. Small is Beautiful: Economics as if People Mattered. New York: Harper & Row, 1989.

[2] Keys, Tracey, Thomas Malnight and Kees van der Graaf. "Making the Most of Corporate Social Responsibility." *McKinsey Quarterly*, December 2009.

[3] van der Graaf, Kees, Tracey Keys and Thomas Malnight. "The Power of Chinese Medicine." *LCF Insights* 2010-003. Lausanne: IMD Global CEO Center: Leading in a Connected Future, 2010.

[4] Ibid.

[5] By Bjarte Hetland (Own work) (CC-BY-3.0 (www.creativecommons.org/licences/by/3.0)) via Wikimedia Commons

Appendices

I: UNILEVER'S EXECUTIVE STRUCTURE

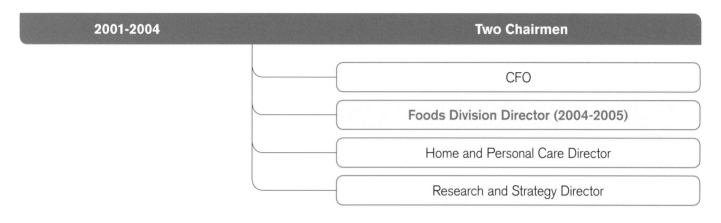

2001-2004	**Two Chairmen**

- CFO
- **Foods Division Director (2004-2005)**
- Home and Personal Care Director
- Research and Strategy Director

2005-2008	**Group Chief Executive**

- **President Europe (2005-2008)**
- President Americas
- President Africa, Middle East, Asia
- Category President Foods
- Category President HPC
- CFO
- Chief HR Officer

Kees van der Graaf's
position at the time

2008 - Present (post Kees)	Group Chief Executive

- President Western Europe
- President Americas
- President Africa, Middle East, Eastern Europe
- Category President
- CFO
- Chief HR Officer
- CSC Officer
- Chief Marketing Officer
- Chief Research Officer

II: MY POSITION IN UNILEVER'S TOP STRUCTURE

1990-1993 Director East Asia Pacific (Board Member)

Foods Member

Foods Directors of the Unilever Countries in the Region

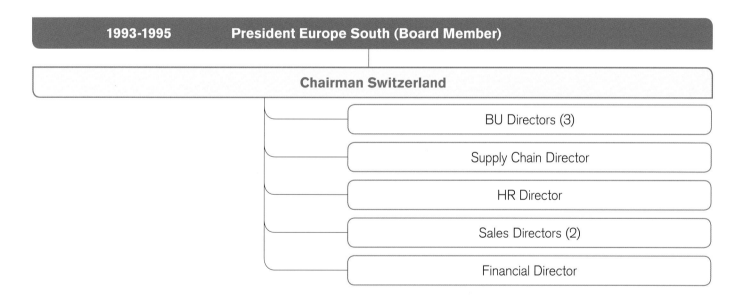

1993-1995   President Europe South (Board Member)

Chairman Switzerland

BU Directors (3)

Supply Chain Director

HR Director

Sales Directors (2)

Financial Director

Kees van der Graaf's
position at the time

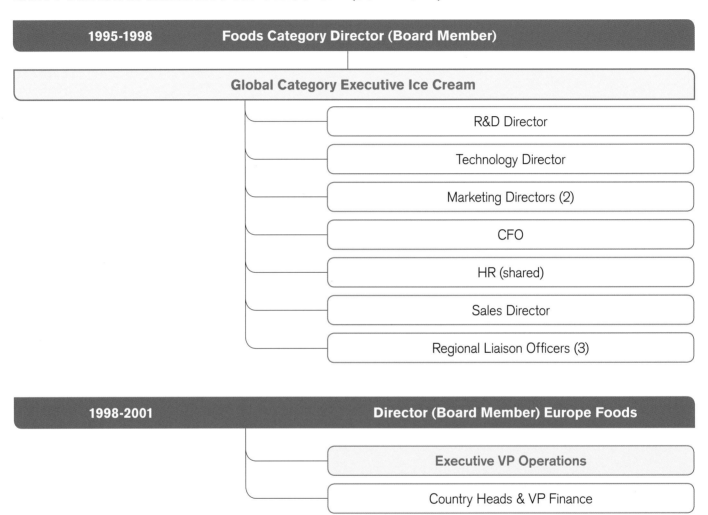

1995-1998	Foods Category Director (Board Member)

Global Category Executive Ice Cream

- R&D Director
- Technology Director
- Marketing Directors (2)
- CFO
- HR (shared)
- Sales Director
- Regional Liaison Officers (3)

1998-2001	Director (Board Member) Europe Foods

- **Executive VP Operations**
- Country Heads & VP Finance

Kees van der Graaf's
position at the time

II: MY POSITION IN UNILEVER'S TOP STRUCTURE (CONTINUED)

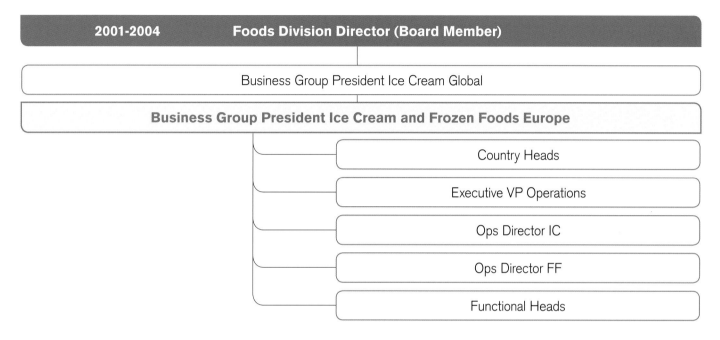

2001-2004	Foods Division Director (Board Member)

Business Group President Ice Cream Global

Business Group President Ice Cream and Frozen Foods Europe

- Country Heads
- Executive VP Operations
- Ops Director IC
- Ops Director FF
- Functional Heads

Kees van der Graaf's
position at the time

II: MY POSITION IN UNILEVER'S TOP STRUCTURE (CONTINUED)

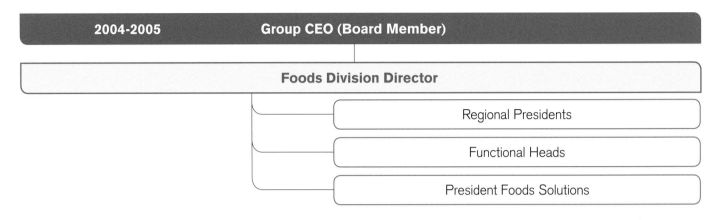

2004-2005	Group CEO (Board Member)

Foods Division Director

- Regional Presidents
- Functional Heads
- President Foods Solutions

2005-2008	Group CEO (Board Member)

President of Europe & Board Member

- Country Heads
- Executive VP Small Countries
- Functional Heads
- Chairman Supply Chain Company

Kees van der Graaf's
position at the time

The FSHD Foundation
Roadmap to Solutions – Strategy 2008–2011

In November 2007 the FSHD Foundation organized a second scientific symposium to discuss the most recent scientific developments in FSHD, review the Roadmap achievements, and develop its research strategy (roadmap) for the next 4–5 years. It was decided that next to continuous support of research that will increase our understanding of the detailed causes of FSHD, our roadmap for the next 5 years should focus on studies that can improve the day-to-day quality of life of FSHD patients.

As a consequence, the 2007–2011 roadmap will focus on the following projects:

- Follow-up studies on aerobic training and fatigue, using additional monitoring tools such as MRI and a web-based personalized monitoring system.
- New comprehensive bioinformatics analysis to gain more detailed insights into the disease mechanism through existing data, via international collaboration.
- Continuation of the effects of oxygen damage and inflammation in FSHD. In this project, the effects of ageing and oxidative stress on progression of the disease and whether diet and lifestyle may slow down this progression will be studied.
- Studies have shown that a change in chromatin structure is central to the FSHD disease mechanism. What still needs to be investigated is the exact determination of the dynamic changes of the chromatin structure in FSHD and what the consequences and modulators of these changes are. With this knowledge we hope to be able to develop possible therapeutic avenues for patients.
- As FSHD is such a rare disease, international standards for clinical and molecular diagnosis and procedures for treatment and care of patients are very important. To realize this, the FSHD Foundation will look into organizing a meeting with all European stakeholders.
- Very recently, two specific genes – FRG1 and DUX4 – were identified as the most important candidates in the cause and progression of FSHD. The FSHD Foundation will continue to support research in this area.

IV: KEES VAN DER GRAAF'S CURRENT ACTIVITIES

IMD _____
- Executive-in-Residence
- Co-Director, IMD Global CEO Center: Leading in a Connected Future

Corporate Boards _____
- ANWB
- Ben & Jerry's
- Carlsberg
- Grandvision BV
- MyLaps
- 3M Holdings

Societal Boards _____
- Founder and Chairman, FSHD Foundation
- Supervisory Board of the Muscles for Muscles Foundation

Other _____
- Consultant, coach, facilitator
- Guest speaker, lecturer

Publications _____
- "Making the most of corporate social responsibility." *McKinsey Quarterly*, December 2009 (with co-authors Tracey Keys and Thomas Malnight).
- "Kericho: A Sustainable Tea Plantation." IMD case no. IMD-3-2080, 2009 (with co-authors Tracey Keys and Thomas Malnight).
- "World Food Program." IMD case no. IMD-3-2081, 2009 (with co-authors Tracey Keys and Thomas Malnight).
- "Unilever Ice Cream Europe." Five-case series on complexity, IMD-3-2082/2086, 2009 (with co-authors Tracey Keys and Thomas Malnight).
- "The Power of Chinese Medicine." *LCF Insights*, 2010-003, IIMD Global CEO Center: Leading in a Connected Future (with co-authors Tracey Keys and Thomas Malnight).
- "Recasting Business around Relationships not Transactions." *LCF Insights*, 2011-002, IMD Global CEO Center: Leading in a Connected Future (with co-author Thomas Malnight).

What others have to say about this book

Paul Polman _____
Chief Executive Officer, Unilever

❝ *Defining Moments is a deeply honest, personal and at times moving account of one man's voyage of self-discovery. Through a series of "defining moments", Kees shows how personal crises and professional challenges can not only be overcome but can also be used to help give greater purpose and meaning to life – to help make the individual stronger, the family more cohesive and the organization more united.* ❞

Annie McKee _____
Founder, Teleos Leadership Institute

❝ *In the midst of the joys, the sorrows, the stress and the excitement of life, it is easy to lose sight of what is most important to us – the people we love, our communities, and the work we care so much about. Kees van der Graaf shares lessons that can help us stay focused and balanced. In Defining Moments, Kees shows us how to seek the sun, even when the sky is dark and clouds gather; how to do the right thing, even when it means taking huge risks; and how to reach for our dreams and help others achieve theirs.* ❞

Peter Killing _____
IMD Professor

❝ *I love this book. It raises fundamental issues about how senior managers make key decisions. The examples in Kees's book range from him spending a week in the countryside with 40 of his managers as they debate and establish key priorities and begin to come together as a team to Kees's sleepless night in a London hotel room, where he made a huge decision – completely on his own – that would change his organization for years to come. The contrast is startling and thought-provoking. And as a teacher of managers – that is what I am looking for in a good management book.* ❞

Poul Weihrauch _____
President, Wrigley Europe

❝ *I enjoyed the read a lot – the personal stories and the theme of holistic life. And I found the insights VERY powerful.* ❞

Lord Simon of Highbury _____
CBE

It's a fascinating story.

James Allen _____
Bain & Company

Great project. Kees continues to amaze me. Always learning and improving.

Thomas Malnight _____
IMD Professor

For me, this book is as much about personal insights and lessons as it is about professional impact. It is about a leader who provides the space and opportunity to work in a different way, a leader who truly engages and empowers the individuals in his organization, and a leader who cares about the impact he has on the organization and the world around him.

Peggy Dulany _____
Founder & Chair, The Synergos Institute

I think Kees expresses in very human terms the dilemma that many people do not allow themselves to confront – feeling trapped in one alternative or another. Because of his position in business, other high-up business people will be interested in reading this book, and I hope that it will open them up to reflecting on their own situations in similar ways.

Sandy Ogg _____
Operating Partner, Portfolio Operations Group, The Blackstone Group
Formerly Chief Human Resources Officer at Unilever

Much has been written about corporate social responsibility and work-life balance. These are two very important ideas that have captured the imagination and energy of many forward-looking organizations. Until now, I was not aware of anyone who had written about (much less practised) the magic of "dynamically balancing" one's energy among family, a major corporation and society in a systematic way.

Real World. Real Learning®

IMD is consistently top ranked among business schools worldwide. With more than 60 years' experience, IMD applies a real world, real learning approach to executive development and offers pioneering and collaborative solutions to address clients' challenges. Its perspective is international – it understands the complexity of the global environment.

Incorporated under the name "International Institute for Management Development," IMD, as the institution is now known, is an independent not-for-profit foundation based in Switzerland. It is funded entirely through its programs, research and partnership activities.

IMD's 60 faculty members, comprising 19 nationalities, are recognized authorities in their fields. They divide their time between teaching, research and consulting. By regularly interacting with executives from major companies around the world, they remain firmly on top of the latest developments in managerial practice. The result is real-impact executive learning and leadership development, which enables IMD participants to learn more, deliver more and be more.

Every year, some 8,000 executives, representing over 98 nationalities, attend more than 21 open-enrollment executive development programs (including intensive MBA and EMBA programs) as well as company-specific partnership programs. Participants come from virtually every sector of the service and manufacturing industries. Cultural backgrounds range from young managers to board members from world-class corporations. English is the working language, though no single business approach dominates.

Learning at IMD has its roots in original IMD research. Currently more than 70 research projects are underway; each led by one or several faculty members. IMD carries out its research and program development in close collaboration with industry. To create value, faculty members not only make sure that research initiatives are relevant to practicing managers, but they also produce a steady flow of new material for IMD programs.

In 2011, IMD launched the first in a series of Global Centers – the IMD Global CEO Center: Leading in a Connected Future. IMD's Global Centers will be focused on thought leadership in areas of interest to key stakeholders. Each Global Center will combine a rigorous research agenda with the development of educational materials and programs for senior level executives.

More than 200 of the world's leading companies have chosen IMD as their preferred learning partner. By joining the IMD Learning Network, companies have access to IMD's latest management research and knowledge. Rapid global access is made available through an annual agenda of webcasts, discovery and leadership events, as well as books and other research publications. Each learning partnership is unique – and is defined and shaped by close interaction between member companies and IMD.

IMD provides ongoing learning opportunities to executives who have participated IMD programs through the IMD Alumni Network, a powerful business network of more than 60,000 executives, which is structured into some 45 active clubs around the world.